*L*Alphonsus *L*iguori

*L*The Redeeming *L*ove of Christ

A Collection of Spiritual Writings

edited by
JOSEPH OPPITZ, C.SS.R.

New City Press

Published in the United States by New City Press
206 Skillman Avenue, Brooklyn, New York 11211
©1992 New City Press, New York

Text selection of chapters I - IV and VI - VIII based on
Tutto spero per il sangue di Cristo (G. Casoli, ed.)
©1982 Città Nuova Editrice, Rome, Italy

Cover design by Nick Cianfarani

Library of Congress Cataloging-in-Publication Data:

Liguori, Alfonso Maria de', Saint, 1696-1787.
    [Tutto spero per il sangue di Cristo. English]
    The redeeming love of Christ / Alphonsus Liguori ; Joseph Oppitz, ed.

    Rev. translation of: Tutto spero per il sangue di Cristo.
    ISBN 0-911782-97-4 : $8.95
    1. Spiritual life—Catholic authors—Early works to 1800.
    I. Oppitz, Joseph W. II. Title.
    BX2349.L55313   1992
    240—dc20
                                                                    91-33543

Printed in the United States of America

Contents

PREFACE

St. Alphonsus exercised an extraordinary influence as a preacher of the gospel and a teacher of prayer. What is the secret behind this unique impact? Ever since I read his spiritual books in my novitiate I asked myself this question.

He speaks from heart to heart. He is filled with enthusiastic and faithful love of Jesus, and that very love gave him an unlimited zeal for salvation: he wanted to see Jesus loved by all people. He shares with his reader this joy of faith, this trust in the saving love of Jesus, his overflowing gratitude for the love Jesus has shown to us all by shedding his blood. Seized by such love and trust Alphonsus felt a holy wrath against the heresy of the Jansenists (widespread at that time even in Naples) who asserted that Jesus spent his blood only for a few elect.

Alphonsus had a loving heart already before he left his career as a lawyer. This becomes evident through one episode. His father did what was usual at that time among the wealthy and noble: he gave his first-born a Turkish slave, a Muslim, for his personal service and protection. Alphonsus never told him that he should become a Christian. Of his own he asked for instruction and baptism with the surprising reason: "If Alphonsus can be so kind and gracious, how good must then be his God whom he loves so much!"

Alphonsus had a brilliant mind and as a lawyer he was a master of the spoken word. But all this would not have made him the great master of spirituality, the Doctor of the Church who so untiringly taught that God calls all people to holiness. Full of this faith he felt a great pain looking back to the time of his worldly career, a time in which he practiced his faith with a kind of mediocrity, as he felt it. Of course, many of us would be happy to be already at that level of "mediocrity."

Jesus himself had called him to a most intimate love. And Alphonsus gave all the space in his heart and mind to this love. This was the prayer of his heart: "Dearest Lord, let your holy love possess me wholly. Lord in this my heart . . . Oh divine love, bliss of all whom you touch with the heavenly flame. Come and enkindle my heart with the glowing fire of purity."

Alphonsus had given all his heart, all his mind and will to Jesus and

7

the Father. Of course this was the work of God's grace. But Alphonsus gave place to it, by *leaving behind* everything that could be an obstacle.

The reader will much better understand his enthusiastic sharing, this urgent invitation to join him on his journey to perfect trust and love if he or she gives special attention to the "leaving behind" (*distacco*) of Alphonsus. This leaving behind characterized his whole apostolate, his preaching missions and retreats, his spiritual writings.

For Alphonsus, there is a threefold leaving behind:

1) He leaves behind a particular kind of "world," the world of the privileged who practiced religion, yes, but looking for their own advantages, dangerously close to using religion for self-exaltation. He leaves behind all the privileges of his social class and swears never to look for honor or privilege in the service of the gospel. And what was the exchange: being free for the redeeming love of Jesus in the service of the poorest and the outcast. Leaving behind a superficial and selfish religion, and more specifically, in joining the love of Jesus to the poorest, the outcast, the sinners, he found fullness in the love of Jesus.

2) Leaving behind his family and its expectations: his father was a successful man of career, a royal admiral, whose greatest ambition was to surpass himself in his first-born Alphonsus. It was easy for the young man Alphonsus to love his tender-hearted mother, but he also loved his father, although he could be very harsh and over-demanding. In order to be totally free for the redeeming love of Jesus, Alphonsus not only disappointed his father greatly by leaving behind any kind of career, but it was a kind of agony when Alphonsus for ever left behind his house, in order to be totally free for the poor.

Having left all this behind Alphonsus became the charismatic teacher of prayer, of trust in Jesus and love of Jesus for the poorest, the *lazzaroni* of Naples. My own efforts to spread the idea of "Houses of Prayer" had a model in Alphonsus' forming among the very poorest of Naples prayerful communities, and neighborhood apostolic groups. The poor themselves became teachers of prayer, integrating life and faith. But even while spending the best of his energies for this apostolate for the poorest and among the poorest of Naples Alphonsus was still for the people the once-famous lawyer, and he was frequently invited to preach in the most illustrious churches, with people of all social classes flocking to his sermons.

3) Convinced that his life-vocation was to preach the good news to the most abandoned, the poorest people far from city-life—we would say far from civilization—he left his beloved Naples and its cultural standard behind in order to live among the poor and for the poorest. *Totally free.* Add to this threefold leaving behind the self-liberation of this fervent apostle from the rigoristic teaching and practice he had been taught in the major seminary of Naples by honest and zealous men. His heart was anguished, he suffered under scrupulosity while turning his mind and will away from all kind of rigorism. It was possible for him because he had left everything behind in favor of proclaiming the good news to the poor. This made it possible for Alphonsus to become at that time "the mildest of all moralists," as popes said of him.

Leaving behind all this, his heart could burn in love for Jesus and for all the redeemed. He is inflamed with love. And in his apostolate of the word and in his writings he shares with us his love, his trust, his unlimited gratitude for the blood of the Redeemer. The more the reader will be aware of this loving person behind his words, the more blissfully he or she will experience this sharing of love by a saint.

While meditating with Alphonsus about the highest price Jesus has paid, his precious blood, in order to manifest his love to us, the plentiful redemption, remember that the saint who speaks to you has also paid his price by "leaving behind" in order to make himself the troubadour of the enchanting love of Jesus.

Bernard Haring, C.SS.R.

INTRODUCTION

Some Biographical Notes

A saint's life is but a living translation of the gospel, and so I shall be explaining the gospel when I speak about St. Alphonsus Liguori. Of all the Doctors of the Church he is the one who has received the title "Most Zealous Doctor." And he is a unique Doctor. Today, of course, we would regard him as a "pastoral" Doctor.

But he was also a man of humor and of easy joy.... As a rule, real joy springs from genuine virtue, of which Alphonsus had plenty. Most of all he had his special love for God and for souls. We might well regard the most devout and useful of his works, The Practice of the Love of Jesus Christ, as in fact his autobiography. It mirrors his own life perfectly especially in the affections and prayers that conclude each chapter. As a matter of fact, nearly all of Alphonsus' works begin and are studded throughout with jewels of devout prayer.

(Albino Luciani—Pope John Paul I,
Pastoral Letter to Clergy of Venice, 1972)

We begin our introduction with these words of the "smiling pope," then cardinal of Venice, because they highlight some of the keynotes of Alphonsus' spirituality. These qualities—his pastoral zeal and love, his down-to-earth practice of that love, his devout prayer and his easy joy in carrying out the will of his beloved Lord—these are the very reasons why we want to share with you some of the gem-like selections from his spiritual writings. They are qualities of an eighteenth century saint but they are just as relevant to us as we approach the start of a new century, striving to make our own life a living translation of the gospel.

For those of you who may not be familiar with the life of Alphonsus Liguori we give a bird's-eye view of the man and his eighteenth century milieu. Each person's spirituality grows, not in a vacuum, but in the complicated concrete matrix of one's own family, cultural, social, political and religious background, hence the importance of some familiarity with Liguori's roots. He was a man thoroughly in touch with his own time and place and the influences of that time and place on his spiritual growth are evident in his life, his work and his writings. It was a long life of almost ninety-one years. He was born in Naples, Italy, in 1696 and he died in Pagani, a small town south of Naples, in 1787.

The father, Giuseppe Liguori, was a naval captain, something of a martinet, a super-perfectionist, a manipulative and domineering father of Alphonsus and his seven brothers and sisters. He demanded quality and performance of all of his children. Papa Liguori was pious in the typically eighteenth century Neapolitan style—greatly devoted to the saints, popular non-liturgical devotions, semi-annual retreats, meditation on the Passion of Christ and a routine of formal prayer and penitential practices. As the oldest child and son, Alphonsus was singled out for a special paternal vigilance; the primogeniture had not only its privileges but also its burdens. The father's influence touched not only his spiritual formation, (he carted the young "Fonsy" with him to the Jesuit and Vincentian retreats), but also every other phase of the young man's growth—hired tutors for a solid humanistic training in languages, music, architecture, philosophy and law. Even Alphonsus' social life came under the rigid control of the father who became matchmaker for the teenaged son; both attempts at marriage engagements failed, thanks to the non-cooperation of young Liguori who had obviously inherited a streak of his father's stubbornness.

The first twenty-seven years of Alphonsus' life show us a young gentleman of the upper nobility, unusually gifted and successful in all of his studies, indeed, a child prodigy. At twelve he was already attending classes at the University of Naples and at sixteen he was a Doctor in both civil and Church law. However, after several years of a brilliant legal practice, he was rather ignominiously humiliated by the loss of a notorious case. He left the courtroom in a fury at what he considered the arbitrary conduct and decision of the court, mumbling to himself, "Ah world, I know you now!" He never returned to the court again.

Throughout these early years of intensive study, the atmosphere often charged by the sparks, and at times lightning and thunder, of the battles between father and son, "Fonsy" was sustained and supported by the tender loving care of his mother, an ever-present counter balance to the rigorous Giuseppe. A woman of both Spanish and Italian blood and convent-educated, she in her own quiet way also left her own mark on the

psychological and spiritual personality of her son. Exceedingly pious, she
seems to have run her home like a miniature novitiate: morning prayers,
spiritual reading time (she too, liked the lives of the saints), noon prayers,
examination of conscience time, night prayers, plus all sorts of assorted
penitential practices suited to the age of the children. She herself practiced
physical mortifications with vigor, even taking the cord-whip discipline.
The religious atmosphere was aided by the presence of a bishop on either
side of the family, namely, Emilio Cavalieri, brother to Mamma Liguori,
bishop of Troia and himself a saintly man, and Domenico Liguori, a
relative of the father. It is my opinion that the young Alphonsus'
scrupulosity and his at times excessive physical mortifications were the
result of his mother's influence on him. She was assisted in the spiritual
formation of her children by Father Tommaso Pagani, a Pious Worker,*
who was a kind of house-chaplain. This man was Liguori's confessor and
spiritual director through Alphonsus' early years, indeed, until the latter
was in his early thirties.

After leaving the practice of the law, Liguori decided on the priesthood,
much to his father's chagrin. Alphonsus had already made a private vow
of celibacy at one of the Vincentian retreats and his movement away from
the high-society lifestyle was definitively confirmed by a unique religious
experience. While still in a quandary over the courtroom debacle, he heard
the voice of the Lord calling him: "Leave the world, and give yourself to
me!" It was not a one-shot experience but was repeated several times; the
locus was the Hospital for Incurables, a place where the young nobleman
performed, as a member of a religious confraternity, weekly service for
the poor. With characteristic promptness and vigor, he made his move, a
decision which brought on another stormy encounter with his father who
had other plans for his son.

Liguori became a priest at the age of thirty and immediately threw
himself into working for the poor and abandoned of the slums of Naples.
It was a real conversion in lifestyle; from the swank salon and the elegant
ballroom, he now moved among the hovels of the fishmongers, the
stevedores, the galley-slaves and the street urchins—that class of society
which we today would call the marginal and abandoned. In a short time

---

* "The Pious Workers" was an association of priests, founded in 1524, made up of priests
who wished to live in common and work together on a special project, in this case,
missions among the poor. They were not "religious" in the full sense of the word since
they took no perpetual public vows in the Church.

he became remarkably popular among the lowest of the *lazzaroni* in the most wretched quarters of the city.

After just about four years of pastoral work Alphonsus, always frail and plagued with health problems, was forced to take a bit of rest and recreation in the purer air of the Amalfi coast. Here, in the mountains above a hillside town called Scala, he underwent a second conversion. He met, for the first time the goatherders, the shepherds and the charcoal makers, the most abandoned mountain folk for whom neither Church nor state seemed to care. He had thought the slums of Naples were bad but here were souls at the very bottom of the pit of abandonment. Alphonsus' response was to found the Congregation of the Most Holy Redeemer, a band of mission preachers with a preferential option for the poor. Everything that he did from that point on, his thirty years of mission-preaching, the 111 books he published, his thirteen years as bishop of a mountain-diocese—all were fired by an intense love for those who needed the good news of the gospels most of all.

In his old age cervical and lumbar arthritis were added to his almost life-long eye problems and his persistent asthma. His head was so bent forward that it wore a wound into his chest and he had to be carried about in a chair. Not being able to preach, read his Office or say Mass was one of the great crosses of his later years and his acceptance of the cross was the supreme carrying out of the prayer which he had written into his stations of the cross: "Grant that I may love you always, and then do with me what you wish!" His last years were spent in Pagani where he remained active almost to the end.

The Writings of Alphonsus Liguori

Those who lived with Liguori were convinced that he had made a vow not to waste a moment of time. His first love was mission-preaching and this primarily for the spiritually abandoned poor. However, he could also be called a model of the apostolate of the pen and his writings, for the most part, were simply an extension of his pastoral zeal. What he said about his *Moral Theology,* a work that would bring him worldwide fame and the title of Doctor of the Church, could truly be applied to all of his theological and ascetical output:

My writing is focused entirely on the practical and is not replete with theoretical questions. I have in mind rather to promote the salvation of souls and therefore I have selected matters that are most useful and practical.

(Moral Theology, Gaude edition, II)

His style was thoroughly persuasive and totally convincing and he had a special genius for bringing the most profound truths of the Catholic faith down to the level of the ordinary folks in his audience. He put this genius and all the quality education he had had to good use for the cause of Christ. The copious redemption proclaimed in the motto he chose for his Congregation was made real in all of his thousands of sermons as well as in the printed works that he published.

Liguori's sources for all that he wrote were first of all the sacred scriptures, then the Fathers of the Church, followed by the writing of the saints and the classical authors within the Catholic tradition. Let me quote Albino Cardinal Luciani once again:

> I mentioned that Alphonsus was a thorough respecter of tradition. In his *Moral Theology* the opinions of eight thousand different theologians are discussed . . . over 34,000 quotations. Despite the careful documentation, each of his works is a sort of pulpit-in-print. Alphonsus marches forth from each book the prophets, the apostles, the great popes, the Doctors, the martyrs, the more illustrious of the spiritual masters especially St. Thomas, St. Francis de Sales and St. Teresa. They rather than Alphonsus do the talking. They, the greats of antiquity, of the middle ages and of modern times are all there . . . in brief Christian tradition.
>
> *(Pastoral Letter to Clergy of Venice)*

In this brief quotation, the soon-to-be pope mentions three out of four of Liguori's favorite saints, that is, Thomas, de Sales and Teresa of Avila. There is one more—Ignatius Loyola.

a. *From Teresa* he inherited the following:

1. her passionate attachment to the humanity of Christ;
2. her sense of practical realism versus the esoteric and ethereal illuminism and otherworldly Quietism of her day which persisted down to his own time;
3. her strong sense of sacramentality;
4. her dogmatic orthodoxy and strong attachment to the popes.

All of these Teresian qualities appear in Liguori's own battles against Quietism and Jansenism and in his many works on the sacraments and on the primacy and infallibility of the Church. His interest in Teresa was a very personal thing; he called her his "second Mamma" (his first mother being Mary Immaculate). Indeed, the *Novena to St. Teresa* was one of his earliest devotional works. His ascetical works abound with Teresian quotations.

b. *The de Sales Influence*

Francis was second only to Teresa as a formative factor in Liguori's own spirituality. In de Sales we see the following characteristics which appear repeatedly in Alphonsus' ascetical writing:

1. a stress on the gratuity and super-abundance of salvation;
2. a stress on the sweetness and tenderness of divine love, with the goal of arousing a reciprocal love on our part;
3. a stress on the divine will even in the ordinary affairs of life, with an appreciation of the supernaturality of the commonplace;
4. a concern for the development of a popular piety for the masses;
5. an acceptance of learning and of the *belles lettres* as allies of holiness.

c. *The Ignatian Element*

There can be no doubt as to the Ignatian factor in Alphonsus Liguori's spiritual growth. He was baptized by a Jesuit; his family entertained Jesuit friends; his youthful retreats were made primarily with the Jesuits; he himself was a frequent guest at the Jesuit Provincial House at Naples; two of his principal advisers in the founding of Liguori's Redemptorists were the Jesuit Fathers Manulio and Pepe. Last but not least we have clear evidence of Alphonsus' deep attachment to the Society in the passionate letter which he wrote to the Holy Father begging him not to suppress the Jesuits and in his deep depression when the tragic deed was done.

From a comparative study of the two great founders, Ignatius and Alphonsus we think that the following characteristics of Ignatian spirituality are most evident in Liguori's own spiritual way:

1. its rootedness in the concept of pastoral service;
2. this spirit of pastoral service is itself rooted in an *effective* love, that is, a love geared toward action rather than toward mystical contemplation;

3. its communitarian apostolicity, demanding corporate order and structure for the sake of mission with this factor at the root of the typical Jesuit *esprit de corps*. Included in this notion would be that of an obedience totally committed to mission;

4. and finally, a common sense prudence with regard to religious experiences. Both Ignatius and Alphonsus were extremely suspicious of the unusual and extraordinary in terms of mystical prayer and mystical phenomena. Both felt that acquired contemplation, not infused contemplation was a call to all men and women with infused contemplation as the "icing on the cake"— nice if it's given by God, but still not necessary for salvation. While both saints did experience extraordinary mystical graces, their respective paths to holiness seemed to have been along the road of the tried and true, the commonplace and the ordinary, bolstered by the universal means of sanctification, that is, active prayer, dynamic pastoral work and the good moral life.

d. *The Aquinas Factor*

Though Liguori's philosophical formation was essentially Cartesian, in theology he was a Thomist at heart. In a brief introduction such as this we will not even attempt to gather together all the quotations from Aquinas and the basically Thomistic doctrines which lie beneath Liguori's own theological stance. Suffice it to say that Liguori leans most heavily on Thomas in his dogmatic works and his *Moral Theology* more so than in his ascetical works, although there is an interesting comparison between Liguori's contemplative teachings and those of St. Thomas and St. John of the Cross, a study published by Garrigou-Lagrange, O.P., under the title *The Love of God and the Cross of Jesus* (St. Louis: Herder, 1951).

Liguori and the Problems of His Time

With the above overview of Liguori's spiritual growth in mind, we can now move on to see how he applied his spiritual teachings to the concrete problems of his day—something that we too must be about in our own troubled times. Like St. Thomas More, Alphonsus was a "man for all seasons." It is true that his geographical perimeters were quite limited; most of his life was spent within the Kingdom of Naples with the exception of a brief trip to Rome for his consecration as bishop of St. Agatha of the Goths and a side trip to the House of Loretto. However, he was a prodigious reader and was well informed of the political, social and religious events that were taking place throughout the continent and beyond. Someone has said that God always raises up a help for the special times of crisis in both Church and state. Alphonsus Liguori was one of the God-sent heroes for several of the crises of the eighteenth century. There were three special nemeses, all of the religious category, which sparked his pastoral concern and led him to his prolific publication in both moral and ascetical theology. The three major crises which he confronted were: first, the sad deterioration of the Church, especially in the Kingdom of Naples, secondly, the growth of Jansenism even in his beloved Italy, and thirdly, moral rigorism in the *cura animarum,* a major pastoral aberration of his day. Some of the selections that you will be reading can only be truly appreciated in the light of the three problems just mentioned.

1. *The Condition of the Church*

For this area of pastoral concern we shall let Liguori speak for himself. The first quote is from a Liguori letter written to Cardinal Castelli who had consulted Alphonsus about a forthcoming papal election.

> To free the Church from this condition of relaxation and decline into which all the classes have fallen, not all the sciences, not even all human prudence will be sufficient. What is needed now is the all powerful arm of God.
>
> Among bishops, there are few who have real zeal for souls; almost all the religious orders are in decay (and we could almost omit the word "almost"), the secular clergy are even worse off. Indeed, a general reform of the clergy is needed so as to remedy the great corruption of the laity.
>
> (General Correspondence #773)

In a subsequent letter to Father Peter-Paul Blasucci, the superior of the Sicilian Redemptorists, Alphonsus lists some of the specific roots of the decay of the Church he loved so well.

> My God, where are we? The young are taught that they should follow the teachings of Jansen and Quesnel. And because of this the learned are thoroughly confused and bewildered. The Age of the

Enlightenment! Yet souls are being lost! Naples is lost! Nobody goes to confession anymore; nobody wants to listen to sermons anymore, and add to this the fact that the laity pretend to decide theological and moral matters by themselves and they criticize everything—scripture, dogma, the precepts etc.

(Special Correspondence #245)

Liguori was not a person who simply sat around bemoaning the spiritual tragedies around him. He was a man of action and his pastorally creative imagination contributed some splendid offerings, not just for the Church of his day; they were contributions which had a lasting effect on the spirituality of the Church even unto our own time. He was convinced that there was a major lacuna in the formation of the clergy especially the rural clergy and so he sat down and wrote his *Moral Theology,* his *Selva* (a book of meditations for the clergy), his *Sunday Sermons,* his *Praxis Confessarii,* plus a book of special guidance for the country-confessor. For the clerics who were inept at Latin, he made a vernacular translation of the psalms. With an eye to correct and edifying Liturgy he also wrote several commentaries on the rubrics of the Mass and there are innumerable letters to both priests and nuns on plain-chant and choral music at the Liturgy. Liguori was also convinced that the ignorance of the laity was due in part to poor catechesis or, in some cases, its complete absence. And so he sat down and wrote both a large and a small catechism for use on parish missions and in every church in his diocese. Moreover, catechesis was made an integral part of the Alphonsian mission system. His zeal for quality education in the Church did not end with the clergy; the nuns also were a special object of his care. He wrote literally hundreds of letters of spiritual direction to nuns throughout the Kingdom of Naples and insisted that quality spiritual direction was a must; better to have none at all than to have mediocre direction. So much for his efforts to bring the Church out of its condition of woeful spiritual mediocrity.

2. *Jansenism*

Liguori's battle with Jansenism was something else again. Jansenism is more than mere absence of due religious formation; with Jansenism we must contend with a perverted religious gnosis, a kind of pseudo-Catholicity, all the more deceptive and dangerous because of an appealing veneer of esoteric piety and selective salvation. It was not something new in Liguori's century but under one form or another had been a thorn in the side of the Church long before Bishop Jansen gave it its name via his *Augustinus* in 1640. Its tenets include a despotic God, selective salvation for but a few of the elite, non-existing free-will, active devotional piety is a useless exercise, holy communion and reconciliation are to be rare experiences, devotion to Mary and the saints are suspect and even dangerous, and finally, and *per consequens* moral and pastoral theology must always be on the side of rigorism.

Each and every one of these tenets of Jansenism fired Liguori's dynamic pen. The selections in this book are but a small sample of his answer to Jansenism: God is a God of love; there is no such thing as selective salvation, rather there is *copious redemption for all* (the Redemptorist motto), all men and women are given the grace to pray and those who pray shall be saved while those who reject that universal grace shall be lost. Active prayer, and not mere passive quietistic prayer, can and should be taught to all and the same is true for devotional piety to the eucharist, to Mary and to the saints. Holy communion and reconciliation are not fearful sacraments reserved for rare occasions in life, indeed, frequent communion and confessional absolution from sin are to be encouraged. Finally, moral rigorism is to be avoided like the black plague of Christian life.

3. *Moral Rigorism*

We shall not devote much space to Liguori's thirty-year-long battle against moral rigorism simply because this book has selections only from his ascetical writings. We must point out, however, that his ascetical masterpiece, *The Practice of the Love of Jesus Christ,* is the very soul of his moral teaching. You cannot begin to appreciate his moral writings and the benign and moderate position they propose—something quite revolutionary in his time of rigid rigorism and wild laxism—unless you understand that he arrived at that moral stance via the gospel way of Christ which is the way of love.

Liguori had had personal experience with the ravages of rigorism in his earlier years. Later in life he admitted that he had been as rigoristic as the best of them, thanks to his teachers and their probabiliorist textbooks. He had lived in terror of damnation and saw sin just about everywhere. The moral message that had been drummed into him was: always play it safe by following the stricter moral opinion. He did not become a free man until his thirties when he began to develop his moral system which he called "Equiprobabilism." Alphonsus' moral system is based on the primacy of liberty; in his *Monitum* of 1772 he says that the primacy of liberty is the very heart of his system. He held that where there are opinions equally probable *pro* and *con*, even when the opinion in favor of the law is slightly more probable, one may still follow the opinion for liberty. And this is true, not because the opinions are equally probable, but because the presence of equally probable opinions make the law truly a doubtful law and doubtful laws do not bind. He likewise insisted that an interior promulgation of the law at the level of individual conscience, a personal interiorization of the law is essential before a law can become binding in conscience. Let's listen to the master with words from his *Apologia* on the *Moderate Use of the Probable Opinion:*

> Although the rigid opinion may be more secure for salvation *per se,* in practice it is not because this would impose on one the danger of formal sin and damnation. There are many things that are safer, but it is also radically safer to believe that one is not obliged to them unless the obligation is clear.

> When we act with moral certitude of the goodness of our acts we are secure in our conscience, for then the danger of formal sin ceases and there remains only the danger of material sin; and this latter danger does not interfere with one's salvation for God condemns only formal sin and not material sin, indeed, so-called material sins are not sins at all. We call them material sins simply because they would supply the matter, the material of sin if such things were done with that kind of advertence necessary to turn them into sins.

For defending this very benign position Alphonsus was accused of being an enemy of the sound moral teaching of Jesus Christ. In typical Neapolitan fashion he responded (again in the *Apologia*):

> *Povero mè.* Poor me! Without knowing it, I am now an opponent of the sound morals of Jesus Christ. Poor me! But nonetheless, I repeat and will always repeat: God has never, and you will not find it in the scriptures, God has never imposed upon any person the command to observe all doubtful laws.

This inflexible stance of Liguori plus his teaching on the primacy of liberty, on the very real possibility of invincible ignorance, even of natural law conclusions, on the necessity of an interior, personal promulgation of law, on leaving people in good faith when and if an instruction would confuse them into the danger of formal sin—all of these Alphonsian tenets lead me to conclude that he was not only the foremost moralist of his time but that he is also a moralist for our own times of confusion, moral doubt, and at times, even despair.

Now you are just about ready to begin the eight selections which we have made for you from the spiritual writings of Alphonsus Liguori. We hope that these little samplers will move you into a deeper study of the works of Liguori. Our selections have been arranged in a coherent order so as to provide you with an integral vision of the various levels of his spiritual way.

1. Love
2. Uniformity with the Divine Will
3. Communicating with God
4. Prayer
5. Meditations
6. The Passion of Christ
7. Preparation for Death
8. Mary.

Each selection will be preceded by a short lead-in so as to help you see the selection in its wider original context.

Joseph Oppitz, C.SS.R.

The translations of St. Alphonsus' writings have been taken from the most recent edition of *The Complete Works of Saint Alphonsus Liguori*, edited by Rev. Eugene Grimm, C.SS.R., with a few minor adjustments. Among which, scripture quotations have been replaced with *The New American Bible*, ©1970 Confraternity of Christian Doctrine, and antiquated English has been updated.

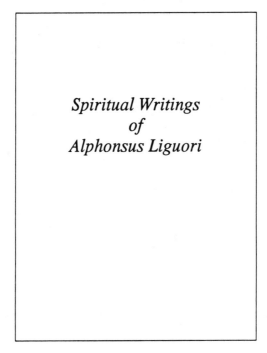

Spiritual Writings
of
Alphonsus Liguori

LOVE, THE PRIMARY THEME
OF LIGUORI'S SPIRITUALITY

Love for God and love for others, plus a special preferential love for the spiritually abandoned poor, was the very heart and soul of the life, the preaching and the writings of Alphonsus Liguori. He writes:

> I recommend that you speak often of the love which God has shown us in the person of Jesus Christ, as seen especially in his passion and in the institution of the eucharist; also speak of the love that we must have for our most holy Redeemer, which we should often recall in these two great mysteries of love.
>
> It is certain that all that is done only out of fear, and not out of love, will have no lasting effects. *(Selva* III, Appendix)

Alphonsus' rule of thumb for advancing in holiness was the same as that of Paul: "Above all, put on love which is the bond of perfection" (Col 3:14). This was the core message of his masterpiece, *The Practice of the Love of Jesus Christ.* The very first page of this work begins with a quote from de Sales: "Some say perfection consists in austerity of life; others in prayer or almsgiving, still others in frequenting the sacraments. They are deceived. Perfection consists of loving God with our whole heart." He had learned this the hard way after thirty years of serving a fearful deity. It was Tommaso Falcoia, who became his spiritual director in the early years of Alphonsus' priesthood, who insisted that he must leave the road of fear once and for all and get onto the road of love. This advice was the lifesaver which kept him from sinking further into the sea of scrupulosity which had plagued him for three score years. Paul's letter to the Corinthians (1:13) supplies the matter for Liguori's tender commentary. However, even if he had never written this magnificent pastoral panegyric on love, we would still be able to conclude that for him love was like the very breath he breathed. There is not one of his ascetical works which does not have a passionate section on God's love for us and our need to love him in return. O admirable exchange—God loves us and we love him.

This was a special characteristic of Alphonsus' love doctrine; namely, the mutuality of love between Beloved and lover, the contra-cambio, the

25

give-and-take and give-in-return which is most perfectly seen in Christ's love and the response of those who become aware of his love.

We must hasten to say that for Liguori, love was not just another virtue in a long catalogue of virtues to be practiced in a methodical or formalistic way. Love was the very *élan vital* of Christian life, a kind of ontological need, as we would say today. The best expression of this is in the marvelous commentary of Achille Desurmont, C.SS.R., one of the greatest authorities on Alphonsian spirituality.

> In people who pursue the spiritual life, you can distinguish two ways. The first strives for the love of God through the virtues. They mortify themselves in a spirit of penance, they practice humility because justice demands it, they obey because duty demands it. These moral virtues are geared toward restoring order in the soul and, little by little, they will lead on to the sphere of perfect charity.
>
> Others take an opposite way. These immediately look to love. This is the virtue they wish to acquire. Therefore, they seek to attain it in the heart of the divine Savior so as to inflame their own hearts. For them, this queen of the virtues is, so to say, the only virtue from which all the others flow so that their whole life arises out of the interior depth of the soul. Love of God in these privileged souls is the point of departure for everything and anything they do. In these people, it is love that does penance, love which practices mortification, humility and submission, it is love that is aflame with zeal, it is love that is patient.
>
> Anytime that circumstances demand this or that particular virtue, love itself suffices to arouse the appropriate virtue-response. They say: "Because I love Jesus, this is why I obey; because I love Jesus, this is why I suffer voluntarily; because I love Jesus, I work with zeal for his honor. My love is a good in which all goods are contained—*unum bonum in quo omnia sunt.*"
>
> St. Alphonsus Liguori belongs to this seraphic school. In it, he is a luminary. He was on fire with love of God and in his old age he could say: "I have found all things in the love of the Redeemer." Through the whole course of his long life, he attained from this love his great zeal, his enlightened prudence, his strong patience; in a word, all the virtues.
>
> (*L'art d'assurer son salut,* in *Oeuvres* I, Introduction)

It is significant that one of Liguori's favorite books of the Old Testament was the Canticle of Canticles, a tender and detailed account of the love-relationship between the lover and the Beloved. Indeed, he himself wrote a commentary on the Canticle, a prayerful commentary to be used in visiting the Blessed Sacrament or as a prayer after holy communion. I have the feeling that the nine qualities of love which he has left us were extracted from his own meditations on the Canticle of Canticles. Here they are as they appear in *The Practice of the Love of Jesus Christ:*

1. It is *"filially fearful"* (*amor timorosus*), that is, it is a childlike love, the love of a child who fears to lose the grasp of the hand of the mother and father it loves; a child who wants to bring only joy to those it loves and is, therefore, fearful lest it bring them disappointment and rejection.

2. It is a *generous love,* and its generosity arouses zeal for deeper expressions of love.

3. It is a *strong love* because it is supported by the passion and cross of Christ. As such, it is sacrificial and long-suffering and persevering in its love despite temptations to the contrary.

4. It is an *obedient love* and this desire to do whatever the Beloved wishes appears in its whole attitude toward authority, in its docility to spiritual guidance, in its seeking for and responding to divine inspiration, and in its unity with the divine will.

5. It is a *pure love,* that is, its motivation is energized by its fixed gaze and focus on its Beloved. (The term *"fixed gaze"* was a favorite of Sister Marie Celeste Crostarosa, Liguori's dear friend in Christ.)

6. It is an *ardent love,* that is, it wants to set the whole world on fire with love and wishes all people to know of the Beloved.

7. It is an *inebriating love,* that is, a love which makes one "crazy with love," almost as if one were drunk with joy over the Beloved's presence and his constant gift-giving, that is, his incarnation, passion, the eucharist, Mary, etc. It is this kind of love which at times leads to the so-called "holy follies" of the great saints, as for example the Redemptorist Brother, St. Gerard Majella.

8. It is a *unitive love* which unites the wills of the Beloved and the one loved. Obviously, as in the Canticle, this brings about an intense yearning to be in the presence of the one loved and an intimacy which is verbal in communicating that love and which is truly alive, especially in the Real Presence of holy communion.

9. It is a *hopeful love,* that is, it is always looking forward to a deepening of the love-relationship here, and hereafter in the final, total, unending, and effortless love in heaven.

These nine qualities of love are contained, at least implicitly, in his methodology of spiritual direction which is most evident in his letters to religious women. I shall summarize them for you:

a. *The first step*

The person must be made aware of God's unsurpassable love for him or her. To this end, all the gospel texts which point to the Father's loving, salvific plan, carried out in Christ and his sacraments, must be marshalled forth and passionately proclaimed. In a word, the authentic image of God as a God of love must be accepted, internalized, and then responded to in the following ways.

b. *The second step*

There then follows a firm decision and deep resolve to take all the positive moves and accept the negative denials that are necessary in a sincere striving for an ever more intimate love-relationship with the Father and his loving will. This is the sacrificial and self-denial aspect of love.

c. *The third step*

The will must be set on fire with ardent desires, a real yearning for an efficacious union of wills, and this involves a constant discerning as to what is God's will. Alphonsus often uses the phrase "to give him pleasure" to express the effect of love's yearning.

d. *The fourth step*

There must be a continual refocusing of the heart on the final goal of total union in heaven. For this purpose Liguori insists upon daily mental prayer with special emphasis on what he called "the eternal truths," namely, the ultimate meaning of human existence as seen in the loving, salvific will of God, the basic options, etc.

The brief selection which follows will touch upon these basics of Alphonsian love. It is what Aquinas called an *amor amicitiae,* a love between friends. ("I no longer call you servants but friends" Jn 15:15.) This love-relationship between a God and his creatures, created in his own image which is love, has its concrete historical expression in the salvific incarnation and passion of Christ and is prolonged in the sacrament of the eucharist. This is why it has been said that the whole of Liguori's spirituality can be summed up in four words: crib, cross, sacrament, and

Mary, she whose relationship with the Father, Son, and Spirit was *the* love-relationship *par excellence.*

Let us sum up all of this in one concise formula: for Alphonsus Liguori, the perfect act of love consists in an unconditional love and surrender to God, for his sake and to the exclusion of all self-interest, and this precisely as a response to his totally unconditional love and surrender to us via the salvific life, death, and resurrection of Jesus, the Redeemer.

The Practice of the Love of Jesus Christ

Who can deny that, of all devotions,* devotion to the passion of Jesus Christ is the most useful, the most tender, the most agreeable to God, one that gives the greatest consolation to sinners, and at the same time most powerfully enkindles loving souls? Whence is it that we receive so many blessings, if it be not from the passion of Jesus Christ? Whence have we hope of pardon, courage against temptations, confidence that we shall go to heaven? Whence are so many lights to know the truth, so many loving calls, so many spurrings to change our life, so many desires to give ourselves up to God, except from the passion of Jesus Christ? The apostle therefore had but too great reason to declare those to be excommunicated who did not love Jesus Christ. "If anyone does not love the Lord, let a curse be upon him" (1 Cor 16:22).

St. Bonaventure says there is no devotion more fitted for sanctifying a soul than meditation on the passion of Jesus Christ; whence he advises us to meditate every day upon the passion, if we would advance in the love of God. "If you would make progress, meditate daily on the passion of the Lord. . . ." And before him St. Augustine, as Bustis relates, said, that one tear shed in memory of the passion is worth more than to fast weekly on bread and water for a year. Wherefore the saints were always occupied in considering the sorrows of Jesus Christ: it was by this means that St. Francis of Assisi became a seraph. He was one day found by a gentleman shedding tears, and crying out with a loud voice: being asked the cause, "I weep," he answered, "over the sorrows and ignominies of my Lord: and what causes me the greatest sorrow is, that people, for whom he suffered so much, live in forgetfulness of him." And on saying this he wept the more, so that this gentleman began also himself to weep. When the saint heard the bleating of a lamb, or saw anything which reminded him of the passion of Jesus, he immediately shed tears. On another occasion, being sick, someone told him to read some pious book. "My book," he replied, "is Jesus crucified." Hence he did nothing but exhort

---

* For St. Alphonsus devotion means a heartfelt, personal and affective love that is manifested through faithfulness.

his brethren to be ever thinking of the passion of Jesus Christ. Tiepoli writes: "He who becomes not inflamed with the love of God by looking on Jesus dead upon the cross, will never love at all."

The Council of Trent says, that in this gift of the eucharist Jesus Christ desired, as it were, to pour forth all the riches of the love he had for humanity. And the apostle observes, that Jesus desired to bestow this gift upon men and women on the very night itself when they were planning his death: "On the night in which he was betrayed, [he] took bread and after he had given thanks, broke it and said: 'This is my body, which is for you' " (1 Cor 11:23, 24). St. Bernardine of Sienna says, that Jesus Christ, burning with love for us, and not content with being prepared to give his life for us, was constrained by the excess of his love to work a greater work before he died; and this was to give his own body for our food.

(*Practice,* Intro I)

St. Philip Neri could find no other name for Jesus Christ in the sacrament save that of "love"; and so, when the holy viaticum was brought to him, he was heard to exclaim, "Behold my love; give me my love. . . ." And who could ever have thought—if he himself had not done it—that the incarnate Word would hide himself under the appearance of bread, in order to become himself our food? "Does it not seem folly," says St. Augustine, "to say, Eat my flesh; drink my blood?" When Jesus Christ revealed to his disciples the sacrament he desired to leave them, they could not bring themselves to believe him; and they left him, saying: "This sort of talk is hard to endure! How can anyone take it seriously?" (Jn 6:60). But that which human beings could neither conceive nor believe, the great love of Jesus Christ has thought of and accomplished. "Take this and eat," said he to his disciples before he went to die; and through them to us all. Receive and eat: but what food shall that be, O Savior of the world, which you desire to give us before you die? "Take this, and eat; this is my body." This is not earthly food; it is I myself who give myself entirely to you.

And in order that everyone might easily receive him, he desired to leave himself under the appearance of bread; for if he had left himself under the appearance of some rare or very costly food, the poor would have been deprived of him; but no, Jesus would hide himself under the form of bread, which costs but little, and can be found everywhere, in order that all in every country might be able to find him and receive him in the holy communion, he not only exhorts us to do so by so many invitations— "Come, eat my food; and drink of the wine I have mixed" (Prv 9:5). "Eat, friends; drink" (Sg 5:1), speaking of this heavenly bread and wine—but he even gives us a formal precept: "Take this, and eat; this is my body." And more than this; that we may go and receive him, he entices us with the promise of paradise. He who feeds on my flesh has life eternal. "Who feeds on this bread shall live forever" (Jn 6:54, 58). And still more, he threatens us with hell, and exclusion from paradise, if we refuse to communicate. "If you do not eat the flesh of the Son of Man, you have no life in you" (Jn 6:53). These invitations, these promises, these threats, all proceed from the great desire he has to come to us in this sacrament.

He stands there as though behind a wall; and from there he peers, as it were, through a closed lattice: "He stands behind our wall, gazing through the windows, peering through the lattices" (Sg 2:9). It is true, we do not see him; but he sees us and is there really present: he is present, in order that we may possess him: but he hides himself from us to make us desire him: and as long as we have not reached our true country, Jesus desires to give himself wholly to us, and to remain united with us.

(*Practice,* Intro II)

"[Let us] persevere in running the race which lies ahead; let us keep our eyes fixed on Jesus, who inspires and perfects our faith. For the sake of the joy which lay before him, he endured the cross, heedless of its shame" (Heb 12:1, 2). Let us go out to the battle with great courage, looking at Jesus crucified, who from his cross offers us his assistance, the victory, and crown. In past times we fell into sin because we left off looking at the wounds and the pains endured by our Redeemer, and so we did not have recourse to him for help. But if for the future we set before our eyes all he has suffered for love of us, and how he ever stands ready to assist us when we have recourse to him, it is certain that we shall not be conquered by our enemies. St. Teresa said, with her wonted generosity, "I do not understand the fears of certain persons, who say, The devil, the devil, so long as we can say, God, God, and make Satan tremble." On the other hand, the saint assures us, that if we do not place all our confidence in God, all our own exertions will be of little or no avail. "All our exertions," these are her own words, "are of little use, if we do not give up entirely all trust in ourselves, and place it altogether in God."

(*Practice*, Intro III)

St. Francis de Sales called Mount Calvary "the mountain of lovers." It is impossible to remember that mount and not love Jesus Christ who died there for love of us.

"Love is a great thing," says St. Bernard. A great thing, a precious thing is love. Solomon, speaking of the divine wisdom, which is holy charity, called it an infinite treasure; because he that possesses charity is made partaker of the friendship of God: "For to men she is an infinite treasure; those who gain this treasure win the friendship of God" (Wis 7:14).

The Angelic Doctor, St. Thomas, says, that charity is not only the queen of all virtues, but that, wherever she reigns, she draws along with her, as it were, in her train, all other virtues, and directs them all so as to bring us in closer union with God; but charity is properly that which unites us with God. As St. Bernard tells us: "Charity is a virtue uniting us with God." And, indeed, it is over and over again signified in the holy scriptures, that God loves whoever loves him: "Those who love me, I also love" (Prv 8:17). "Anyone who loves me . . . my Father will love him; we will come to him, and make our dwelling place with him" (Jn 14:23). "Who abides in love abides in God, and God in him" (1 Jn 4:16). Behold the beautiful union which charity produces; it unites the soul to God. Moreover, love supplies strength to practice and to suffer everything for God: "Stern as death is love" (Sg 8:6). St. Augustine writes: "Nothing is so hard that it cannot be subdued by the fire of love." Wherefore the saint says, that where we love, either the labor is not felt, or if felt, the labor itself is loved: "In that which is loved, either there is no labor, or the labor is loved."

Let us hear from St. John Chrysostom what are the effects of divine love in those souls in which it reigns: "When the love of God has taken possession of a soul, it produces an insatiable desire to work for the Beloved; insomuch that however many and however vast the works which she does, and however prolonged the duration of her service, all seems nothing in her eyes, and she is afflicted at doing so little for God; and were it permitted her to die and consume herself for him, she would be most happy. Hence it is that she esteems herself an unprofitable servant in all that she does; because she is instructed by love to know what God deserves, and sees by this clear light all the defects of her actions, and finds in them motives for confusion and pain, well aware how mean is all that she can do for so great a Lord."

(*Practice,* Intro IV)

Let us hear what St. John Chrysostom says of a soul wholly given up to almighty God: "He who has attained the perfect love of God seems to be alone on the earth—he no longer cares either for glory or ignominy—he scorns temptations and afflictions—he loses all relish and appetite for created things. And as nothing in this world brings him any support or repose, he goes incessantly in search of his beloved without ever feeling wearied; so that when he toils, when he eats, when he is watching, or when sleeping, in every action and word, all his thoughts and desires are fixed upon finding his beloved; because his heart is where his treasure is."

(Practice I)

People of the world look on things with many eyes, that is, have several inordinate views in their actions; as for instance, to please others, to become honored, to obtain riches, and if nothing else, at least to please themselves; but the saints have but a single eye, with which they keep in view, in all that they do, the sole pleasure of God; and with David they say: "Whom else have I in heaven? And when I am with you the earth delights me not" (Ps 73:25, 26).

And here we must remark, that we must not only perform good works, but we must perform them well. In order that our works may be good and perfect, they must be done with the sole end of pleasing God. This was the admirable praise bestowed on Jesus Christ: "He has done everything well" (Mk 7:37). Many actions may in themselves be praiseworthy, but from being performed for some other purpose than for the glory of God, they are often of little or no value in his sight. St. Mary Magdalene of Pazzi said, "God rewards our actions by the weight of pure intention." As much as to say, that according as our intention is pure, so does the Lord accept and reward our actions. But, O God, how difficult it is to find an action done solely for you! I remember a holy old man, a religious, who had labored much in the service of God, and died in the reputation of sanctity; now one day, as he cast a glance back at his past life, he said to me in a tone of sadness and fear, "Woe is me! When I consider all the actions of my past life, I do not find one done entirely for God."

Those who have nothing else in view in their undertakings than the divine will, enjoy that holy liberty of spirit which belongs to the children of God; and this enables them to embrace everything that pleases Jesus Christ, however revolting it may be to their own self-love or human respect. The love of Jesus Christ establishes his lovers in a state of total indifference; so that all is the same to them, be it sweet or bitter; they desire nothing for their own pleasure, but all for the pleasure of God. With the same feelings of peace, they address themselves to small and great works; to the pleasant and the unpleasant: it is enough for them if they please God.

Many, on the other hand, are willing to serve God, but it must be in such an employment, in such a place, with such companions, or under such circumstances, or else they either quit the work, or do it with an ill will. Such persons have not freedom of spirit, but are slaves of self-love and on that account gain very little merit by what they do; they lead a troubled life, because the yoke of Jesus Christ becomes a burden to them. The true lovers of Jesus Christ care only to do what pleases him; and for the reason that it pleases him when he wills, and where he wills, and in the manner he wills: and whether he wishes to employ them in a state of life honored by the world, or in a life of obscurity and insignificance. This is what is meant by loving Jesus Christ with a pure love; and in this we ought to exercise ourselves, battling against the craving of our self-love, which would urge us to seek important and honorable functions, and such as suit our inclinations.

(Practice III)

The tepidity, then, that does hinder perfection is that tepidity which is avoidable when a person commits deliberate venial faults; because all these faults committed with open eyes can effectually be avoided by the divine grace, even in the present life. Wherefore St. Teresa said: "May God deliver you from deliberate sin, however small it may be." Such, for example, are willful untruths, little detractions, imprecations, expressions of anger, derisions of one's neighbor, cutting words, speeches of self-esteem, animosities nourished in the heart, inordinate attachments to persons of a different sex. "These are a sort of worm," wrote the same saint, "which is not detected before it has eaten into the virtues." Hence, in another place, the saint gave this admonition: "By means of small things the devil goes about making holes for great things to enter. . . ."

All the evil arises from the little love they have for Jesus Christ. Those who are puffed up with self-esteem; those who frequently take to heart occurrences that fall out contrary to their wishes; who practice great indulgence toward themselves on account of their health; who keep their heart open to external objects, and the mind always distracted, with an eagerness to listen to, and to know, so many things that have nothing to do with the service of God, but merely serve to gratify private curiosity; who are ready to resent every little inattention from others, and consequently are often troubled, and grow remiss in prayer and recollection. One moment they are all devotion and joy, the next all impatience and melancholy, just as things happen, according to or against their humor; all such persons do not love Jesus Christ, or love him very little, and cast discredit on true devotion.

But suppose we should find ourselves sunk in this unhappy state of tepidity, what do we have to do? Certainly it is a hard thing for a soul grown lukewarm to resume her ancient fervor; but our Lord has said, that what human beings cannot do, God can very well do. "Things that are impossible for men are possible for God" (Lk 18:27). Whoever prays and employs the means is sure to accomplish his desire.

The means to cast off tepidity, and to tread in the path of perfection, are five in number: 1. the desire of perfection; 2. the resolution to attain it; 3. mental prayer; 4. frequent holy communion; 5. prayer.

The first means, then, is the desire of perfection. Pious desires are the wings which lift us up from earth; for, as St. Laurence Justinian says, desire "supplies strength, and renders pain more light": on the one hand it gives strength to walk toward perfection, and on the other hand it lightens the fatigue of the journey.

Many are called to perfection; they are urged on toward it by grace, they conceive a desire of it; but because they never really resolve to acquire it, they live and die in the ill-odor of their tepid and imperfect life. The desire of perfection is not enough, if it be not followed up by a stern resolve to attain it. How many souls feed themselves on desires alone, but never make withal one step in the way of God! It is of such desires that the wise man speaks when he says: "The sluggard's propensity slays him!" (Prv 21:25). The sluggard is ever desiring, but never resolves to take the means suitable to his state of life to become a saint. He says: "Oh, if I were but in solitude, and not in this house! Oh, if I could but go and reside in another monastery, I would give myself entirely up to God!" And meanwhile he cannot support a certain companion; he cannot put up with a word of contradiction; he is dissipated about many useless cares; he commits a thousand faults of gluttony, of curiosity, and of pride; and yet he sighs out to the wind: "Oh, if I had but!" or "Oh, if I could but!" etc.

Such desires do more harm than good; because some regale themselves upon them, and in the meantime go on leading a life of imperfection. It was a saying of St. Francis de Sales: "I do not approve of a person who, being engaged in some duty or vocation, stops to sigh for some other kind of life than is compatible with his actual position, or for other exercises unfitted for his present state; for it merely serves to dissipate his heart, and makes him languish in his necessary duties."

We must, therefore, desire perfection, and resolutely take the means toward it. St. Teresa says: "God only looks for one resolution on our part, and will afterwards do all the rest himself: the devil has no fear of irresolute souls."

(Practice IV)

It was the saying of St. Teresa, "Don't think you have advanced far in perfection, till you consider yourself the worst of all, and desire to be placed below all." And on this maxim the saint acted, and so have done all the saints; St. Francis of Assisi, St. Mary Magdalene of Pazzi, and the rest, considered themselves the greatest sinners in the world, and were surprised that the earth sheltered them, and did not rather open under their feet to swallow them up alive; and they expressed themselves to this effect with the sincerest conviction. The Venerable Father John of Avila, who, from his earliest infancy had led a holy life, was on his deathbed; and the priest who came to attend him said many sublime things to him, taking him for what indeed he was, a great servant of God and a learned man; but Father Avila thus spoke to him: "Father, I pray you to make the recommendation of my soul, as of the soul of a criminal condemned to death; for such I am." This is the opinion which saints entertain of themselves in life and death.

We, too, must act in this manner, if we would save our souls, and keep ourselves in the grace of God till death, reposing all our confidence in God alone. The proud rely on their own strength, and fall on that account; but the humble, by placing all their trust in God alone, stand firm and fall not, however violent and multiplied the temptations may be; for their watchword is: "In him who is the source of my strength I have strength for everything" (Phil 4:13). The devil at one time tempts us to presumption, at another time to diffidence; whenever he suggests to us that we are in no danger of falling, then we should tremble the more; for were God but for an instant to withdraw his grace from us, we are lost. When, again, he tempts us to diffidence, then let us turn to God, and thus address him with great confidence: "In you, O Lord, I take refuge; let me never be put to shame" (Ps 31:2). My God, in you I have put all my hopes; I hope never to meet with confusion, nor to be bereft of your grace. We ought to exercise ourselves continually, even to the very last moments of our life, in these acts of diffidence in ourselves and of confidence in God, always beseeching God to grant us humility.

But it is not enough, in order to be humble, to have a lowly opinion of ourselves, and to consider ourselves the miserable beings that we really are; the person who is truly humble, says Thomas à Kempis, despises himself, and wishes also to be despised by others. This is what Jesus Christ so earnestly recommends us to practice, after his example: "Learn from me, for I am gentle and humble of heart" (Mt 11:29). Those who style themselves the greatest sinners in the world, and then are angry when others despise them, plainly show humility of tongue, but not of heart. St. Thomas Aquinas says, that persons who resent being slighted may be certain that they are far distant from perfection, even though they should work miracles.

(Practice V)

The saying of St. Francis of Assisi is most true: "What I am before God, that I am." Of what use is it to pass for great in the eyes of the world, if before God we be vile and worthless? And on the contrary, what matters it to be despised by the world, provided we be dear and acceptable in the eyes of God? St. Augustine thus writes: "The approbation of one who praises neither heals a bad conscience, nor does the reproach of one who blames wound a good conscience." As the one who praises us cannot deliver us from the chastisement of our evil doings, so neither can the one who blames us rob us of the merit of our good actions. "What does it matter," says St. Teresa, "though we be condemned and reviled by creatures, if before you, O God we are great and without blame?" The saints had no other desire than to live unknown, and to pass for contemptible in the estimation of all. Thus writes St. Francis de Sales: "But what wrong do we suffer when people have a bad opinion of us, since we ought to have such of ourselves?"

(Practice VI)

The mistake is, that some indeed wish to become saints, but after their own fashion, they would love Jesus Christ, but in their own way, without forsaking those diversions, that vanity of dress, those delicacies in food: they love God, but if they do not succeed in obtaining such or such an office, they live discontented; if, too, they happen to be touched in point of esteem, they are all on fire; if they do not recover from an illness, they lose all patience. They love God; but they refuse to let go that attachment for the riches, the honors of the world, for the vainglory of being reckoned of good family, of great learning, and better than others. Such as these practice prayer, and frequent holy communion; but inasmuch as they take with them hearts full of earth, they derive little profit. Our Lord does not even speak to them, for he knows that it is but a waste of words. In fact, he said as much to St. Teresa on a certain occasion: "I would speak to many souls, but the world keeps up such a noise about their ears, that my voice would never be heard by them. Oh, that they would retire a little from the world!"

David longed to have wings free from all lime of worldly affections, in order to fly away and repose in God: "Had I wings like a dove, I would fly away and be at rest" (Ps 55:7). Many souls would wish to see themselves released from every earthly trammel to fly to God, and would in reality make lofty flights in the way of sanctity, if they would but detach themselves from everything in this world; but whereas they retain some little inordinate affection, and will not use violence with themselves to get rid of it, they remain always languishing on in their misery, without ever so much as lifting a foot from the ground. St. John of the Cross said: "The soul that remains with her affections attached to anything, however small, will, notwithstanding many virtues which she may possess, never arrive at divine union; for it signifies little whether the bird be tied by a slight thread or a thick one: since, however slight it may be, provided she does not break it, she remains always bound, and unable to fly. . . ." For this reason the ancient Fathers of the desert were accustomed first to put this question to any youth who desired to associate with them: "Do you bring an empty heart, that the Holy Spirit may fill it?"

(Practice VII)

Let us listen to the beautiful lessons given on this subject by that master of meekness St. Francis de Sales: "Never put yourself in a passion, nor open the door to anger on any pretext whatever; because, when once it has gained an entrance, it is no longer in our power to banish it, or moderate it, when we wish to do so. The remedies against it are: 1. to check it immediately, by diverting the mind to some other object, and not to speak a word. 2. to imitate the apostles when they beheld the tempest at sea, and to have recourse to God, to whom it belongs to restore peace to the soul. 3. if you feel that, owing to your weakness, anger has already got footing in your breast, in that case do yourself violence to regain your composure, and then try to make acts of humility and of sweetness toward the person against whom you are irritated; but all this must be done with sweetness and without violence, for it is of the utmost importance not to irritate the wounds." The saint said that he himself was obliged to labor much during his life to overcome two passions which predominated in him, namely, anger, he avowed it had cost him twenty-two years' hard struggle. As to the passion of love, he had succeeded in changing its object, by leaving creatures, and turning all his affections to God. And in this manner the saint acquired so great an interior peace, that it was visible even in his exterior; for he was invariably seen with a serene countenance and a smile on his features. "Where do the conflicts and disputes among you originate? Is it not your inner cravings?" (Jas 4:1). When we are made angry by some contradiction, we fancy we shall find relief and quiet by giving vent to our anger in actions, or at least in words: but we are mistaken, it is not so; for after having done so, we shall find that we are much more disturbed than before. . . . The Holy Spirit says: "Discontent lodges in the bosom of a fool" (Eccl 7:9). Anger remains a long time in the heart of fools, who have little love for Jesus Christ; but if by stealth it should ever enter into the hearts of the true lovers of Jesus Christ, it is quickly dislodged, and does not remain. A soul that cordially loves the Redeemer never feels in a bad humor, because, as she desires only what God desires, she has all she wished for, and consequently is ever tranquil and well-balanced. The divine will tranquilizes her in every misfortune that occurs; and thus she is able at all times to observe meekness toward all. But we cannot acquire this meekness without a great love for Jesus Christ. In fact, we know by experience that we are not meeker and gentler toward others, except when we feel an increased tenderness toward Jesus Christ.

(Practice VIII)

St. Teresa says: "Those persons are deceived who fancy that union with God consists in ecstasies, raptures, and sensible enjoyments of him. It consists in nothing else than in submitting our will to the will of God; and this submission is perfect when our will is detached from everything, and so completely united with that of God, that all its movements depend solely on the will of God. This is the real and essential union which I have always sought after, and continually beg of the Lord." And then she adds: "Oh, how many of us say this, and seem to ourselves to desire nothing besides this; but, miserable creatures that we are, how few of us attain to it!" Such, indeed, is the undeniable truth; many of us say: O Lord! I give you my will, I desire nothing but what you desire; but, in the event of some trying occurrence, we are at a loss how to yield calmly to the divine will. And this is the source of our continually complaining that we are unfortunate in the world, and that we are the butt of every misfortune; and so of our dragging on an unhappy life.

If we were conformed to the divine will in every trouble, we should undoubtedly become saints, and be the happiest of humankind. This, then, should form the chief object of our attention, to keep our will in unbroken union with the will of God in every occurrence of life, be it pleasant or unpleasant. It is the admonition of the Holy Spirit. "Winnow not with every wind." Some people resemble the weathercocks, which turn about every wind that blows; if the wind is fair and favorable to their desires, they are all gladness and condescension; but if there blow a contrary wind, and things fall out against their desires, they are all sadness and impatience; this is why they do not become saints, and why their life is unhappy, because, in the present life, adversity will always befall us in a greater measure than prosperity.... The friends of St. Vincent of Paul said of him while he was still on earth: "Vincent is always Vincent." By which they meant to say, that the saint was ever to be seen with the same smiling face, whether in prosperity or in adversity; and was always himself, because, as he lived in the total abandonment of himself to God, he feared nothing and desired nothing but what was pleasing to God.

"Never consider yourselves," said St. Francis de Sales, "to have arrived at the purity which you ought to have, as long as your will is not cheerfully obedient, even in things the most repulsive, to the will of God."

(Practice IX)

Ah, yes! to the hearts that fervently love Jesus Christ, pains and ignominies are most delightful. And thus we see the holy martyrs going with gladness to encounter the sharp prongs and hooks of iron, the plates of glowing steel and axes. The martyr St. Procopius thus spoke to the tyrant who tortured him: "Torment me as you like; but know at the same time, that nothing is sweeter to the lover of Jesus Christ than to suffer for his sake." St. Gordius, Martyr, replied in the same way to the tyrant who threatened him death: "You threaten me with death; but I am only sorry that I cannot die more than once for my own beloved Jesus." And I ask, did these saints speak thus because they were insensible to pain or weak in intellect? "No," replies St. Bernard, "not insensibility, but love caused this." They were not insensible, for they felt well enough the torments inflicted on them; but since they loved God, they esteemed it a great privilege to suffer for God, and to lose all, even life itself, for the love of God.

St. Teresa wrote this admirable maxim: "Whoever aspires to perfection must beware of ever saying: *They had no reason to treat me so.* If you will not bear any cross but one which is founded on reason, then perfection is not for you."

(Practice X)

Those who believe only with the understanding, but not with the will, as is the case with sinners who are perfectly convinced of the truths of the faith, but do not choose to live according to the divine commandments— such as these have a very weak faith; for had they a more lively belief that the grace of God is a priceless treasure, and that sin, because it robs us of this grace, is the worst of evils, they would assuredly change their lives. If, then, they prefer the miserable creatures of this earth to God, it is because they either do not believe, or because their faith is very weak. On the contrary, those who believe not only with the understanding, but also with the will, so that they not only believe, but have the will to believe in God, the revealer of truth, from the love he has for them, and rejoices in so believing—such persons have a perfect faith, and consequently seek to make their lives conformable to the truths that they believe.

Weakness of faith, however, in those who live in sin, does not spring from the obscurity of faith; for though God, in order to make our faith more meritorious, has veiled the objects of faith in darkness and secrecy, he has at the same time given us so clear and convincing evidence of their truth, that not to believe them would argue not merely a lack of sense, but sheer madness and impiety. The weakness of the faith of many persons is to be traced to their wickedness of living. They who, rather than forgo the enjoyment of forbidden pleasures, scorn the divine friendship, would wish there were no law to forbid, and no chastisement to punish, their sins; on this account they strive to blind themselves to the eternal truths of death, judgment, and hell, and of divine justice; and because such subjects strike too much terror into their hearts, and are too apt to mix bitterness in their cup of pleasure, they set their brains to work to discover proofs, which have at least the look of plausibility; and by which they allow themselves to be flattered into the persuasion that there is no soul, no God, no hell, in order that they may live and die like the brute beasts, without laws and without reason.

And this laxity of morals is the source whence have issued, and still issue daily, so many books and systems of materialists, indifferentists, politicists, deists, and naturalists; some among them deny the divine existence, and some the divine providence, saying that God, after having created human beings takes no further notice of them, and is heedless whether they love or hate him, whether they be saved or lost; others, again, deny the goodness of God, and maintain that he has created numberless souls for hell, becoming himself their tempter to sin, that so they may damn themselves, and go into everlasting fire, to curse him there forever.

(Practice XI)

Thus we see that the desire to go and see God in heaven, not so much for the delight which we shall experience in loving God, as for the pleasure which we shall afford God by loving him, is pure and perfect love. Nor is the joy of the blessed in heaven any hindrance to the purity of their love; such joy is inseparable from their love; but they take far more satisfaction in their love of God than in the joy that it affords them. Someone will perhaps say: But the desire of a reward is rather a love of concupiscence than a love of friendship. We must therefore make a distinction between temporal rewards promised by human beings distinct from their own persons and independent of them, since they do not bestow themselves, but only their goods, when they would remunerate others; on the contrary, the principal reward which God gives to the blessed is the gift of himself: "I am your shield. I will make your reward very great" (Gn 15:1).

(Practice XII)

In order to live always well, we must store up deeply in our minds certain general maxims of eternal life, such as the following:

All passes away in this life, whether it be joy or sorrow; but in eternity nothing passes away.

What good is all the greatness of this world at the hour of death?

All that comes from God, whether it be adverse or prosperous, all is good, and is for our welfare.

We must leave all, to gain all.

There is no peace to be found without God.

To love God and save one's soul is the one thing needful.

We need only be afraid of sin.

If God be lost, all is lost.

Who desires nothing in this world is master of the whole world.

Who prays is saved, and who prays not is damned.

Let me die, and give God pleasure.

Whatever price God asks, is never too much.

Every pain is slight to who has deserved hell.

Who looks on Jesus crucified bears all.

Everything becomes a pain that is not done for God.

Whoever wishes for God alone is rich in every good.

Happy the person who can say: "My Jesus, I desire you alone, and nothing more!"

Who loves God, finds pleasure in everything; who loves not God, finds no true pleasure in anything.

(Practice XIII)

UNIFORMITY WITH THE DIVINE WILL

For Alphonsus Liguori, uniformity with the divine will is simply the other side of the coin of love. Even human lovers are constantly trying to find out what their beloved wants and then they do it simply to give the other party pleasure. This is Liguori's theme-song not only in the *Uniformity With the Divine Will* book, but also in every other ascetical work.

As Dionysius the Areopagite says, the principal effect of love is to unite the will of the lovers so that they may have but one heart and one will. Hence all our actions, our works of penance, our communions and our alms-deeds please God only to the degree that they are conformable with the divine will. If they are not, they are not good works.

(Preparation for Death XXXVI)

Now since the concrete object of Alphonsus' love is the Word incarnate, he insists that we must learn the process of putting on Jesus Christ so that we, as lovers, reach the Pauline goal: "I live now, not I, but Christ lives in me. For me to live is Christ" (Gal 2:20). Here is uniformity at its best. And so, as we read the gospels, we must especially focus on Christ's own constant uniting of his human will with the divine.

It is not to do my own will that I have come down from heaven, but to do the will of him who sent me. (Jn 6:38)

Whoever does the will of my heavenly Father is brother and sister and mother to me. (Mt 12:50)

Your will be done on earth as it is in heaven. (Mt 6:10)

My Father, if it be possible, let this cup pass me by. Still let it be as you would have it, not as I. (Mt 26:39)

None of those who cry out, "Lord, Lord," will enter the kingdom of God, but only the one who does the will of my Father in heaven. (Mt 7:21)

Alphonsus likewise appeals for a study of the saints since they provide role models for this integration of the human with the divine will. Of

45

course, our efforts in this direction will remain only a striving as long as we are still here on earth since only the blessed in heaven love God and are united to him perfectly.

In his *Preparation for Death,* Liguori lines up a practical list concerning the matters in which we should conform ourselves to God's will. It is also here that he lays down an eminently practical distinction, namely, the distinction between the *general will of God* and the *special will of God.* The general will of God requires that we do those things which seem morally good and lawful; with this he sees no great difficulty. The special will of God, however, is an indication of God's will in special cases and entails a limitation or prohibition of the use of our own freedom. This results in duty, obligation, and command. It is my conviction that Liguori held that uniformity with the will of God is a demand only with the order of what pertains to perfection and not to mere counsels. However, an authentic lover would desire to be pleasing to God in all things to the best of his or her ability. He writes:

> It is necessary to conform ourselves to the will of God not only in crosses and adversities which come *directly* from God, such as infirmities, desolation of spirit, loss of relatives or property, but also in those that come *indirectly* from him, such as defamation, contempt, injuries, and persecution, all of which come from other people. It is certain that whatever happens takes place by the divine will. "Good and evil, life and death, poverty and riches, are from the Lord" (Sir 11:14).
>
> *(Preparation for Death* XXXVI)

But is such an attitude really possible? Only in the light of total surrender to the Beloved. As the saint repeats over and over again, there is no one better able to promote our welfare or who loves us more than our Creator.

> Let us be persuaded that whatever he does he does for our good and because he loves us. Many things appear to us to be misfortunes, but if we understood the purpose for which God sends them, we should see that they are really graces. St. Teresa used to say that God never sends a cross without rewarding it with some favor when we accept it with resignation.
>
> *(True Spouse* 14)

We are back to where we started: a loving God and our need to love him in return, a trusting love that brings union of mind and heart. Obviously, like Mary herself, we are allowed to wonder and even question the "how-shall-this-be" aspect of whatever he wills, but the bottom line must always be, "Be it done unto me according to your word"—the very same Marian sentiment which echoed even in the agony in the garden.

We have a marvelous expression of Liguori's own uniformity with the divine will in his stations of the cross. Fourteen times in a row he courageously petitions the Lord: "Grant that I may love you always and then do with me as you wish." And anyone who knows the life of Liguori also knows that the Lord took him at his word.

Conformity to the Will of God

Our whole perfection consists in loving God, who is in himself most lovely: love is the bond of perfection (cf. Col 3:16). But, then, all perfection in the love of God consists in the union of our own with his most holy will. This, indeed, is the principal effect of love; as St. Dionysius the Areopagite observes, "such a union of the will of those who love as makes it to become one and the same will." And therefore the more united a person is with the divine will, so much greater will be his love. It is quite true that mortifications, meditations, communions, and works of charity toward others are pleasing to God. But where is this the case? When they are done in conformity to his will; for otherwise, not only does he not approve them, but he abominates and punishes them. Suppose that there are two servants, one of whom labors hard and incessantly throughout the day, but will do everything after his own fashion; while the other does not work so much, but acts always in obedience to orders: is it not certain that the latter, and not the former, is the one who pleases his master? In what respect do any works of ours serve to the glory of God, where they are not done according to his good pleasure? It is not sacrifices that the Lord desires, says the prophet to Saul, but obedience to his will: "Does the Lord desire holocausts and victims, and not rather that the voice of the Lord should be obeyed?" (1 Kgs 15:22). To refuse to obey is like the crime of idolatry. Who will act from his own will, independently of that of God, commits a kind of idolatry; since in that case, instead of worshipping the divine will, he worships, in a certain sense, his own.

The greatest glory, then, that we can give to God is the fulfillment in everything of his holy will. This is what our Redeemer, whose object in coming upon earth was the establishment of the glory of God, principally came to teach us by his example. See how St. Paul makes him address his eternal Father: "Sacrifice and offering you did not desire, but a body you have prepared for me . . . then I said, 'I have come to do your will, O God' " (Heb 10:5-7).

A single act of perfect conformity to the divine will is sufficient to make one a saint. Look at Saul, whom Jesus Christ illuminates and converts, while he is going on in his persecution of the Church. What does Saul do? What does he say? He simply makes an offering of himself to do the divine will: Lord, what do you want me to do? And, behold, the Lord declares him to be a vessel of election and apostle of the Gentiles: "This man is the instrument I have chosen to bring my name to the Gentiles" (Acts 9:15). Yes, for he who gives his will to God gives him everything: he who gives him his goods in alms, his blood by disciplines, his food by fasting, gives to God a part of what he possesses; but he who gives him his will gives him the whole; so that he can say to him, Lord, I am poor, but I give you all that is in my power; in giving you my will, there remains nothing for me to give you. But this is precisely all that our God claims from us: "My son, give me your heart" (Prv 23:26). My son, says the Lord to each of us—my son, give me your heart; that is to say, your will. "There is no offering," says St. Augustine, "that we can make to God more acceptable to himself than to say to him, Take possession of us." No, we cannot offer to God anything more precious than by saying to him, Lord, take possession of us; we give our whole will to you; make us understand what it is that you desire of us, and we will perform it.

If, then, we would give a full satisfaction to the heart of God, we must bring our own will in everything into conformity with his; and not only into conformity, but into uniformity, too, as regards all that God ordains. Conformity signifies the conjoining of our own will to the will of God; but uniformity signifies, further, our making of the divine and our own will one will only, so that we desire nothing but what God desires, and his sole will becomes ours. This is the sum and substance of that perfection to which we ought to be ever aspiring; this is what must be the aim of all our works, and of all our desires, meditations, and prayers. For this we must invoke the assistance of all our patron saints and of our guardian angels, and, above all, of our divine mother Mary, who was the most perfect of all the saints, for the reason that she ever embraced most perfectly the divine will.

(Conformity I)

But the chief point lies in our embracing the will of God in all things which befall us, not only when they are favorable, but when they are contrary to our desires. When things go on well, even sinners find no difficulty in being in a state of conformity to the divine will; but the saints are in conformity also under circumstances which run counter and are mortifying to self-love. It is herein that the perfection of our love for God is shown. The Venerable Father John Avila used to say, "A single 'Blessed be God,' when things go contrary, is of more value than thousands of thanksgivings when they are to our liking."

Moreover, we must bring ourselves into conformity to the divine will, not only as regards those adverse circumstances which come to us directly from God—such, for instance, as infirmities, desolations of spirit, poverty, the death of parents, and other things of a similar nature—but also as regards those which come to us through the instrumentality of people, as in the case of contumelies, reproaches, acts of injustice, thefts, and persecutions of every kind. On this point, we must understand that when we suffer injury from anyone in our reputation, our honor, or our property, although the Lord does not will the sin which such a one commits, he nevertheless does will our humiliation, our poverty, and our mortification. It is certain and of faith, that everything that comes to pass in the world comes to pass through the divine will: "I form the light and create the darkness, I make well-being and create woe" (Is 45:7). From God come all things that are good and all things that are evil; that is to say, all things that are contrary to our own liking, and that we falsely call evil; for, in truth, they are good, when we receive them as coming from his hands: "If evil befalls a city, has not the Lord caused it?" (Am 3:6), said the prophet Amos. And the Wise Man said it before: "Good things and evil, life and death, are from God" (Eccl 11:14). It is true, as I observed above, that whenever anyone unjustly treats you in an injurious manner, God does not will the sin which such a person commits, nor concur in the malice of his intentions; but he quite concurs, with a general concurrence, as regards the material action by which such a one wounds, plunders, or injures you; so that what you have to suffer is certainly willed by God, and comes to you from his hands. Hence it was that the Lord told David that he was the author of the injuries which Absalom would inflict upon him, even to the taking away of his wives in his very presence; and that in punishment for his sins. Hence, too, he told the Jews that it would be as a punishment for their wickedness when he should have commanded the Assyrians to spoil and bring them to ruin: "Woe to Assyria! My rod in anger . . . I order him to seize plunder, carry off loot" (Is 10:6), which St. Augustine explains, "The wickedness of these people is made to be, as it were, an axe of God." God uses the iniquity of the Assyrians, like an axe, to chastise the Jews.

And Jesus himself said to St. Peter that his passion and death did not come
to him so much from people, as from his Father himself: "Am I not to
drink the cup the Father has given me?" (Jn 18:11).

(*Conformity* II)

Who acts in this way does not only become a saint, but enjoys, even in
this world, a perpetual peace. . . . When cold or heat, rain or wind, prevails,
he or she who is in a state of union with the divine will says, I wish it to
be cold, I wish it to be hot; I wish the wind to blow, the rain to fall, because
God wishes it so. Does poverty, persecution, sickness, death arrive, I also
wish (says such a one) to be poor, persecuted, sick; I wish even to die,
because God wishes it thus.

This is the beautiful liberty that the sons and daughters of God enjoy,
worth more than all the domains and all the kingdoms of this world. This
is that great peace that the saints experience, which surpasses all understanding (cf. Phil 4:7), with which all the pleasures of the senses, all
gaieties, festivities, distinctions, and all other worldly satisfactions, cannot compete; for these, being, as they are, unsubstantial and transitory,
although, while they last, they may be fascinating to the senses, nevertheless do not bring contentment, but affliction, to the spirit wherein true
contentment resides: so that Solomon, after having enjoyed such worldly
pleasures to the full, cried out, in his affliction, "This also is vanity and a
chase after the wind" (Eccl 4:16).

The fool—that is to say, the sinner—changes like the moon, which
today grows, tomorrow wanes. Today you will see him laughing, tomorrow weeping; today all gentleness, tomorrow furious like the tiger. And
why so? Because his contentment depends on the prosperity or the
adversity that he meets with; and therefore he varies as the circumstances
which befall him vary. Whereas the just are like the sun, ever uniform in
their serenity under whatever circumstances may come to pass; because
their contentment lies in their uniformity to the divine will, and therefore
they enjoy a peace that nothing can disturb.

(*Conformity* III)

The holy Abbot Nilus used to say that we ought never to pray to God
that he would accomplish our own will. And whenever, too, things that
are contrary befall us, let us accept them all, as from God's hands, not
merely with patience, but with joy, as did the apostles when they "left the
Sanhedrin full of joy that they had been judged worthy of ill-treatment for

the sake of the Name" (Acts 5:41). And what greater satisfaction can a soul enjoy than in the knowledge that by suffering with a good will anything that it may have to suffer it gives to God the greatest pleasure that it can give him? The masters of the spiritual life teach that, though the desire which certain souls have of suffering to give him pleasure is acceptable to him, he is yet more pleased with the conformity of those who wish for neither joy nor pain, but, in perfect resignation to his holy will, have no other desire than to fulfil whatever that will may be.

(Conformity IV)

But let us now look at the matter from a more practical point of view, and consider what things there are in which we have to bring ourselves into uniformity to the will of God.

In the first place, we must have this uniformity as regards those things of nature that come to us from without; as when there is great heat, great cold, rain, scarcity, pestilence, and the like. We must take care not to say, What intolerable heat! what horrible cold! what a misfortune! how unlucky! what wretched weather! or other words expressive of repugnance to the will of God. We ought to will everything to be as it is, since God is he who orders it all. St. Francis Borgia, on going one night to a house of the Society when the snow was falling, knocked at the door several times; but, the fathers being asleep, he was not let in. They made great lamentations in the morning for having kept him so long waiting in the open air; but the saint said that during that time he had been greatly consoled by the thought that it was God who was casting down upon him those flakes of snow.

In the second place, we must have this conformity as regards things that happen to us from within, as in the sufferings consequent on hunger, thirst, poverty, desolations, or disgrace. In all, we ought ever to say, "Lord, be it yours to make and to unmake. I am content; I will only what you will."

(Conformity V/1)

In the third place, if we have any natural defect either in mind or body—a bad memory, slowness of apprehension, mean abilities, a crippled limb, or weak health—let us not therefore make lamentation. What were our deserts, and what obligation had God to bestow upon us a mind more richly endowed, or a body more perfectly framed? Could he not have created us mere brute animals? or have left us in our own nothingness?

Who is there that ever receives a gift and tries to make bargains about it? Let us, then, return him thanks for what, through a pure act of his goodness, he has bestowed upon us; and let us rest content with the manner in which he has treated us. Who can tell whether, if we had had a larger share of ability, stronger health, or greater personal attractions, we should not have possessed them to our destruction? How many there are whose ruin has been occasioned by their talents and learning, of which they have grown proud, and in consequence of which they have looked upon others with contempt — a danger which is easily incurred by those who excel others in learning and ability! How many others there are whose personal beauty or bodily strength have furnished the occasions of plunging them into innumerable acts of wickedness! And, on the contrary, how many others there are who, in consequence of their poverty, or infirmity, or ugliness, have sanctified themselves and been saved; who, had they been rich, strong, or handsome, would have been damned! And thus let us ourselves rest content with that which God has given us: "One thing only is required" (Lk 10:42). Beauty is not necessary, nor health, nor sharpness of intellect; that which alone is necessary is our salvation.

(Conformity V/2)

In the fourth place, we must be particularly resigned under the pressure of corporal infirmities; and we must embrace them willingly, both in such a manner, and for such a time, as God wills. Nevertheless, we ought to employ the usual remedies; for this is what the Lord wills also: but if they do us no good, let us unite ourselves to the will of God, and this will do us much more good than health. O Lord! let us then say, I have no wish either to get well or to remain sick: I will only that which you will. Certainly the virtue is greater, if, in times of sickness, we do not complain of our sufferings; but when these press heavily upon us, it is not a fault to make them known to our friends, or even to pray to God to liberate us from them. I am speaking now of sufferings that are severe; for, on the other hand, there are many who are very faulty in this, that on every trifling pain or weariness they would have the whole world come to compassionate them, and to shed tears around them. Even Jesus Christ, on seeing the near approach of his most bitter passion, manifested to his disciples what he suffered: "My heart is nearly broken with sorrow" (Mt 26:38); and he prayed the eternal Father to liberate him from it: "My Father, if it be possible, let this cup pass me by" (Mt 26:39). But Jesus himself has taught us what we ought to do after praying in like manner; namely, straightway to resign ourselves to the divine will, adding, as he did, "Still, let it be as you would have it, not as I" (Mt 26:39).

I call the time of sickness the touchstone by which spirits are tried, because in it is ascertained the value of the virtue of which anyone stands possessed. If we do not lose our tranquillity, if we make no complaints, and are not over-anxious, but obey our medical advisers and our superiors, preserving throughout the same peacefulness of mind, in perfect resignation to the divine will, it is a sign that we possess great virtue. But what, then, ought one to say of sick persons who lament and say that they receive but little assistance from others; that their sufferings are intolerable; that they can find no remedy to do them good; that their doctors are ignorant; at times complaining even to God that his hand presses too heavily upon them? St. Bonaventure relates, in his *Life of St. Francis,* that when the saint was suffering pains of an extraordinary severity, one of his religious, who was somewhat over-simple, said to him, "Father, pray to God to treat you with a little more gentleness; for it seems that he lays his hand upon you too heavily." St. Francis, on hearing this, cried aloud, and said to him in reply, "Listen; if I did not know that these words of yours were the offspring of mere simplicity, I would never see you more—daring, as you have done, to find fault with the judgments of God." And after saying this, extremely enfeebled and emaciated through his sickness though he was, he threw himself from his bed upon the floor and kissing it, he said, "Lord, I thank you for all the sufferings which you sent me. I pray to you to send me more of them, if it so pleases you. It is my delight for you to afflict me, and not to spare me in the least degree, because the fulfillment of your will is the greatest consolation which in this life I can receive."

(Conformity V/3)

Moreover, we ought to be resigned in times of spiritual desolation. The Lord is accustomed, when a soul gives itself up to the spiritual life, to heap consolations upon it, in order to wean it from the pleasures of the world; but afterwards, when he sees it more settled in spiritual ways, he draws back his hand, in order to make proof of its love, and to see whether it serves and loves him unrecompensed, while in this world, with spiritual joys. "While we are living here," as St. Teresa used to say, "our gain does not consist in any increase of our enjoyment of God, but in the performance of his will." And in another passage: "The love of God does not consist in tenderness, but in serving him with firmness and humility." And again, elsewhere: "The Lord makes trial of those who love him by means of drynesses and temptations." Let, then, the soul thank the Lord when he caresses it with sweetnesses; but not torment itself by acts of impatience, when it beholds itself left in a state of desolation. This is a point which should be well attended to; for some foolish persons, seeing themselves in a state of aridity, think that God may have abandoned them; or, again, that the spiritual life was not made for them; and so they leave off prayer, and lose all that they have gained. There is no time better for exercising our resignation to the will of God than that of dryness. I am not saying that you will not suffer pain on seeing yourself bereft of the sensible presence of your God; it is impossible for a soul not to feel such pain as this; nor can it refrain from lamentation, when our Redeemer himself upon the cross made lamentation on this account: "My God, my God, why have you forsaken me?" (Mt 27:46).

And what is said with regard to aridity must also be said of temptations. We ought to try to avoid temptations; but if God wills or permits that we be tempted against the faith, against purity, or against any other virtue, we ought not to complain, but resign ourselves in this also to the divine will. To St. Paul, who prayed to be released from his temptation to impurity, the Lord made answer, "My grace is enough for you" (2 Cor 12:9). And so, if we see that God does not listen to us, by releasing us from some troublesome temptation, let us likewise say, Lord, do and permit that which pleases you; your grace is enough for me; only grant me your assistance, that I may never lose it. It is not temptations, but the consenting to temptations, that is the cause of our loss of divine grace. Temptations, when we overcome them, keep us more humble, gain for us greater merits, make us have recourse to God more frequently; and thus keep us further from offending him, and unite us more closely to his holy love.

(Conformity V/5)

Lastly, we must unite ourselves to the will of God in regard to our death, and as to the time and the manner in which he will send it. St. Gertrude one day, when climbing up a hill, slipped and fell into a ravine. Her companions asked her afterwards whether she would not have been afraid to die without the sacraments? The saint answered, "It is my great desire to die with the sacraments; but I consider that the will of God is more to be accounted of, because I hold that the best disposition one could have for dying a good death would be one's submission to that which God might will; consequently, I desire whatever death my Lord shall be pleased to allot me."

(Conformity V/6)

Finally, even as regards our degrees in grace and glory we must bring our own will into conformity to the divine. Highly as we ought to value the things of the glory of God, we ought to value his will yet more. It is right for us to desire to love him more than the Seraphim do, but it is not right for us to go on to wish for any other degree of love than that which the Lord has determined on granting us.

(Conformity V/7)

In short, we ought to regard all things that do or will happen to us as proceeding from God's hand; and everything that we do we ought to direct to this one end, the fulfillment of his will, and to do it simply because God wills it to be done. And in order to go on with greater security in this, we must follow the guidance of our superiors as regards what is external, and of our directors with regard to what is internal, that so we may, through them, understand what it is that God desires of us, having great faith in those words of Jesus Christ to us: "Who hears you, hears me" (Lk 10:16). And, above all, let it be our study to serve God in the way in which it is his will that we should serve him. I say this, that we may shun the deception practiced upon himself by one who loses his time, amusing himself by saying, "If I were in a desert, if I were to enter into a monastery, if I were to go somewhere, so as not to remain in this house, to a distance from these relatives or these companions of mine—I would sanctify myself; I would do such and such penance; I would say such and such prayers." He says, "I would do, I would do"; but in the meantime, through bearing with a bad will the cross which God sends him—in short, through not walking in the way that God wills for him—he not only does not sanctify himself, but goes on from bad to worse. These desires are temptations of the devil, at such times when they are not in accordance with the will of God; we must therefore drive them away, and brace ourselves up to the service of God in that one way which he has chosen for us. By doing his will, we shall certainly sanctify ourselves in any state wherein God places us. Let us, then, ever will only that which God wills, so that he may take and press us to his heart; and, for this end, let us make ourselves familiar with some of those passages of scripture that call upon us to unite ourselves ever more and more to the divine will: "Lord, what do you want me to do?" My God, tell me what you desire of me; for I desire to do it all. "I am yours; save me" (Ps 119:94). O my Lord! I am no longer my own, but yours; do with me whatsoever you please. And at such times especially as when any very grievous calamity befalls us—as in the case of the death of parents, of the loss of property, and things of a similar kind—"Father, it is true" (let it ever be ours to say), "Father it is true—You have graciously willed it so" (Mt 11:26). Yes, my God and my Father, let it be even so; for so it has pleased you. And, above all, let us love that prayer which Jesus Christ has taught us: "Your will be done on earth as it is in heaven." The Lord told St. Catharine of Genoa that whenever she said the Our Father, she was to pay particular attention to these words, and pray that his holy will might be fulfilled by her with the same perfection with which it is fulfilled by the saints in heaven. Let us, too, act in this manner, and we shall certainly become saints ourselves.

(Conformity VI)

COMMUNICATING WITH GOD

This and the next two sections deal with a subject dear to the heart of Alphonsus; namely, communication with God, conversing continually and familiarly with God. *How to Converse Continually and Familiarly with God* is the very title of the book from which the following selection has been taken. He also published a much larger work called *The Great Means of Salvation,* which is, of course, prayer. As we have said about the love and uniformity themes in Liguori's works, so too with prayer! There is no work in the ascetical collection of Alphonsus which does not contain his prayer doctrine. Because of his mammoth output on this topic, he has correctly been called "The Doctor of Prayer."

His motivation for what, at times, seems an obsession with this topic was multiple. Firstly, it is impossible to present the fundamental Christian relationship with God as a love-relationship between lovers without expecting actual, continual, and familiar communication between those lovers. Have you ever stood waiting by a telephone booth which was occupied by a lover calling his beloved? How many times have mothers and fathers of engaged sons and daughters cried out, usually in vain: "Will you get off that phone?" Lovers are the best communicators in the world, morning, noon, and night; their tender verbiage is unlimited. This is Liguori's main reason for wanting to share with all the world his own moving convictions on how to fulfill the gospel invitation to pray and to pray always. Nor does he merely provide theological doctrine, which he surely does with great expertise, but he also lets us share in his own most intimate conversations with Jesus, his Beloved. Almost every chapter in each and every ascetical work ends with a prayer, and that is the standard Alphonsian methodology. A quote from Albino Cardinal Luciani will be appropriate here:

> About his *Great Means of Prayer,* St. Alphonsus himself wrote: "I would like to have printed enough copies so that every Christian in the world might have one." His *Visits to the Blessed Sacrament and to the Blessed Virgin* enjoyed and continue to enjoy colossal success due to the fact that apart from a few ingenious illustrations, they constitute a magnificent series of conversations with Jesus

Christ, conversations held by a man who knew how to talk earnestly and lovingly with Christ. Up until 1933 *The Visits* had had 2,009 editions, of which 265 were in Italian, 861 in French, 165 in Spanish, 324 in German, 184 in Dutch, and 175 in various other languages.

St. Alphonsus is, indeed, the apostle of prayer. He claims that prayer is as necessary to the life of the soul as breathing is to the life of the body. Someone has referred to the bipolarity in the life of Alphonsus: Love and prayer—prayer to draw God within our hearts, and love that we might give ourselves to him. The above is my notion of what forms the heart and soul of Alphonsus' life and work.

(Pastoral Letter to Clergy of Venice)

Liguori's second great motive for writing so extensively on prayer was his desire to put an end to the terrible devastation brought about by the dour heresy of Jansenism. It is impossible to talk about his prayer doctrine without getting into the dogmatic questions of grace, free-will, predestination, and God's loving mercy. His *Great Means* was a frontal attack on the errors of Jansenism on salvation as well as on the loveless legacy of Calvin, Luther, and Wycliff. Then, too, there was the doctrine of stingy salvation propagated by a bastardized Thomism of Domingo Banez, O.P. The result of these heresies was an almost two hundred year patrimony of a kind of heartless and hopeless Christian life. Finally, in the eighteenth century, it was Liguori who stood up and said: "Enough is enough!"

When speaking of his prayer doctrine, we ought to keep in mind that his principal concern was not with the dogmatic polemic but with the pastoral consequences of a faulty prayer theory. He narrows the scope of his own works on prayer by treating those errors which have an adverse effect on the truths which were central to his own spirituality and his theology of copious redemption, namely, God's loving and salvific plan of redemption in and through Christ the Redeemer and his continual gift of sufficient grace to be saved in the form of the gift of the ability to pray. Even the unlettered goatherders of the mountains of Southern Italy—and, perhaps, they most of all—could be taught how to converse continually and familiarly with God. On every Mission and Renewal that he preached he always gave special attention to praying with the people and even leading them into mental prayer.

Even a quick glance at the chapter headings of *How to Converse Continually and Familiarly with God* should convince you of Liguori's gentle persuasion in terms of how to pray. Here are a few of those headings:

1. God, on his part, wishes us to speak to him with confidence and familiarity.

2. It is easy and agreeable to entertain one's self with God.

3. Of what, when, and how we should converse with God. (Here he answers the perennial question of why talk to God when he already knows our needs, indeed, knows all about us.) The what-to-say is summed up in the following titles:

    a. our trials and troubles;

    b. our joys;

    c. our faults and failures;

    d. our doubts;

    e. our neighbors;

    f. our desire for heaven;

    g. our thanks for his love;

    h. our desire for more love of him and his Son and his mother.

4. God always answers the soul that speaks to him.

Then, the *How to Converse* . . . ends with the usual Alphonsian practical summary dealing with the liturgy, mental prayer, the rosary, visiting the Blessed Sacrament, holy communion, the practice of the presence of God within us, and other ways that help keep us in continual conversation with God.

The Way to Converse Always and Familiarly with God

Consider, you have no friend nor brother, nor father nor mother, nor spouse nor lover, who loves you more than your God. The divine grace is that great treasure whereby we vilest of creatures, we servants, become the dear friends of our Creator himself: "For to men she is an unfailing treasure; those who gain this treasure win the friendship of God" (Wis 7:14). For this purpose he increases our confidence; he "emptied himself" (Phil 2:7), and brought himself to nought, so to speak; abasing himself even to becoming man and conversing familiarly with us. . . . He went so far as to become an infant, to become poor, even so far as openly to die the death of a malefactor upon the cross. He went yet farther, even to hide himself under the appearance of bread, in order to become our constant companion and unite himself intimately to us: "The man who feeds on my flesh and drinks my blood remains in me, and I in him" (Jn 6:56). In a word, he loves you as much as though he had no love but toward yourself alone. For which reason you ought to have no love for any but for himself. Of him therefore, you may say, and you ought to say, "My lover belongs to me and I to him" (Sg 2:16). My God has given himself all to me, and I give myself all to him; he has chosen me for his beloved, and I choose him, of all others, for my only love: "My lover is radiant and ruddy; he stands out among thousands" (Sg 5:10).

Accustom yourself to speak with him alone, familiarly, with confidence and love, as to the dearest friend you have, and who loves you best.

(Converse I)

If it be a great mistake, as has been already said, to converse mistrustfully with God—to be always coming before him as a slave, full of fear and confusion, comes before his prince, trembling with dread—it would be a greater one to think that conversing with God is but weariness and bitterness. No, it is not so: "For association with her involves no bitterness and living with her no grief" (Wis 8:16). Ask those souls who love him with a true love, and they will tell you that in the sorrows of their life they find no greater, no truer relief, than in a loving converse with God.

Now this does not require that you continually apply your mind to it, so as to forget all your employments and recreations. It only requires of you, without putting these aside, to act toward God as you act on occasion toward those who love you and whom you love.

Your God is ever near you, nay, within you: "In him we live and move and have our being" (Acts 17:28). There is no barrier at the door against any who desire to speak with him; nay, God delights that you should treat with him confidently. Treat with him of your business, your plans, your griefs, your fears—of all that concerns you. Above all, do so (as I have said) with confidence, with open heart. For God is not wont to speak to the soul that speaks not to him; forasmuch as, if it be not used to converse with him, it would little understand his voice when he spoke to it. And this is what the Lord complains of: "Our sister is little: what shall we do for our sister when her courtship begins?" (Sg 8:8) Our sister is but a child in my love; what shall we do to speak to her if she understand me not? God will have himself esteemed the Lord of surpassing power and terribleness, when we despise his grace; but, on the contrary, he will have himself treated with as the most affectionate friend when we love him; and to this end he would have us often speak with him familiarly and without restraint.

Friends in the world have some hours in which they converse together, and others during which they are apart; but between God and you, if you wish, there shall never be one hour of separation: "When you lie down, you need not be afraid, when you rest, your sleep will be sweet" (Prv 3:24). You may sleep, and God will place himself at your side, and watch with you continually. . . . When you take your rest, he departs not from beside your pillow; he remains thinking always of you, that when you wake in the night he may speak to you by his inspirations, and receive from you some act of love, of oblation, of thanksgiving; so as to keep up even in those hours his gracious and sweet converse with you. Sometimes also he will speak to you in your sleep, and cause you to hear his voice, that on waking you may put in practice what he has spoken: "In dreams will I speak to him" (Nm 12:6).

He is there also in the morning, to hear from you some word of affection, of confidence; to be the depository of your first thoughts, and of all the actions which you promise to perform that day to please him; of all the griefs, too, which you offer to endure willingly for his glory and love. But as he fails not to present himself to you at the moment of your waking, fail not you, on your part, to give him immediately a look of love, and to rejoice when your God announces to you the glad tidings that he is not far from you, as once he was by reason of your sins; but that he loves you, and would be beloved by you: and at that same moment he gives you the gracious precept, "Therefore, you shall love the Lord, your God, with all your heart" (Dt 6:5).

(Converse II)

Say not, But where is the need of disclosing to God all my wants, if he already sees and knows them better than I? True, he knows them; but God makes as if he knew not the necessities about which you do not speak to him, and for which you seek not his aid. Our Savior knew well that Lazarus was dead, and yet he made as if he knew it not, until Magdalene had told him of it, and then he comforted her by raising her brother to life again.

When therefore, you are afflicted with any sickness, temptation, persecution, or other trouble, go at once and beseech him, that his hand may help you. It is enough for you to present the affliction before him; to come in and say, "Look O Lord, upon my distress" (Lam 1:20). He will not fail to comfort you, or at least to give you strength to suffer that grief with patience; and it will turn out a greater good to you than if he had altogether freed you from it. Tell him all the thoughts of fear or of sadness that torment you; and say to him, My God, in you are all my hopes; I offer to you this affliction, and resign myself to your will; but you take pity on me—either deliver me out of it, or give me strength to bear it. And he will truly keep with you that promise made in the gospel to all those who are in trouble, to console and comfort them as often as they have recourse to him: "Come to me, all you who are weary and find life burdensome, and I will refresh you" (Mt 11:28).

He will not be displeased that in your desolations you should go to your friends to find some relief; but he wills you chiefly to have recourse to himself. At all events, therefore, after you have applied to creatures, and they have been unable to comfort your heart, have recourse to your Creator, and say to him, Lord, people have only words for me; my friends are full of words (cf. Jb 6:25); they cannot comfort me, nor do I any more desire to be comforted by them; you are all my hope, all my love. From you only will I receive comfort; and let my comfort be, on this occasion, to do what pleases you. Behold me ready to endure this grief through my whole life, through all eternity, if such be your good pleasure. Only you help me.

Fear not that he will be offended if you sometimes gently complain, and say to him, "Why, O Lord, do you stand aloof?" (Ps 10:1). You know, Lord, that I love you and desire nothing but your love; in pity help me, and forsake me not. And when the desolation lasts long, and troubles you exceedingly, unite your voice to that of Jesus in agony and dying on the cross, and beseech his mercy, saying, "My God, my God, why have you forsaken me?" (Mt 27:46). But let the effect of this be to humble you yet more at the thought that he deserves no consolations who has offended God; and yet more to enliven your confidence, knowing that God does all things, and permits all, for your good: "All things work together for the good of those who have been called according to his decree" (Rom 8:28). Say with great courage, even when you feel most troubled and disconsolate: "The Lord is my light and my salvation; whom should I fear?" (Ps 27:1).

Further, when you receive pleasant news, do not act like those unfaithful, thankless souls who have recourse to God in time of trouble, but in time of prosperity forget and forsake him. Be as faithful to him as you would be to a friend who loves you and rejoices in your good; go at once and tell him of your gladness, and praise him and give him thanks, acknowledging it all as a gift from his hands; and rejoice in that happiness because it comes to you of his good pleasure. Rejoice, therefore, and comfort yourself in him alone: "Yet will I rejoice in the Lord" (Hb 3:18); "let my heart rejoice in your salvation" (Ps 13:6). Say to him, My Jesus, I bless, and will ever bless you, for granting me so many favors, when I deserved at your hands not favors, but chastisements for the affronts I have given you. Say to him with the sacred spouse, "Both fresh and mellowed fruits, my lover, I have kept in store for you" (Sg 7:14). Lord, I give you thanks; I keep in memory all your bounties, past and present, to render you praise and glory for them forever and ever.

Another mark of confidence highly pleasing to your most loving God is this: that when you have committed any fault, you be not ashamed to go at once to his feet and seek his pardon. Consider that God is so greatly inclined to pardon sinners that he laments their perdition, when they depart far from him and live as dead to his grace. Therefore does he lovingly call them, saying, "Why should you die, O house of Israel? Return and live" (Ez 18:31). He promises to receive the soul that has forsaken him, so soon as she returns to his arms: "Return to me. . . and I will return to you" (Zec 1:3). Oh, if sinners did but know with what tender mercy the Lord stands waiting to forgive them! "Yet the Lord is waiting to show you favor, and he rises to pity you" (Is 30:18). Oh, did they but know the desire he has, not to chastise, but to see them converted, that he may embrace them, that he may press them to his heart! He declares: "As I live, says the Lord God, I swear I take no pleasure in the death of the wicked man, but rather in the wicked man's conversion, that he may live" (Ez 33:11). "Come now, let us set things right, says the Lord: Though your sins be like scarlet, they may become white as snow" (Is 1:18).

That you may not lose courage at such a moment, cast a glance at Jesus on the cross; offer his merits to the eternal Father; and thus hope certainly for pardon, since he "did not spare his own son" (Rom 8:32). Say to him with confidence, "Look upon the face of your anointed" (Ps 84:10). My God, behold your Son, dead for my sake; and for the love of that Son forgive me. Attend greatly, devout soul, to the instruction commonly given by masters of the spiritual life, after your unfaithful conduct, at once to have recourse to God, though you have repeated it a hundred times in a day; and after your falls, and the recourse you have had to the Lord (as has been just said), at once to be in peace. Otherwise, while you remain cast down and disturbed at the fault you have committed, your converse with God will be small; your trust in him will fail; your desire to love him grow cold; and you will be little able to go forward in the way of the Lord. On the other hand, by having immediate recourse to God to ask his forgiveness, and to promise him amendment, your very faults will serve to advance you further in the divine love. Between friends who sincerely love each other it often happens that when one has displeased the other, and then humbles himself and asks pardon, their friendship thereby becomes stronger than ever. Do you likewise; see to it that your very faults serve to bind you yet closer in love to your God.

In any kind of doubtfulness also, either on your own account or that of others, never leave acting toward your God with a confidence like to that of faithful friends, who consult together on every matter. So do you take counsel with himself, and beseech him to enlighten you that you may decide on what will be most pleasing to him.

(*Converse* III)

In a word, if you desire to delight the loving heart of your God, be careful to speak to him as often as you are able, and with the fullest confidence that he will not disdain to answer and speak with you in return. He does not, indeed, make himself heard in any voice that reaches your ears, but in a voice that your heart can well perceive,when you withdraw from converse with creatures, to occupy yourself in conversing with your God alone: "I will lead her into the desert, and speak to her heart" (Hos 2:16). He will then speak to you by such inspirations, such interior lights, such manifestations of his goodness, such sweet touches in your heart, such tokens of forgiveness, such experience of peace, such hopes of heaven, such rejoicings within you, such sweetness of his grace, such loving and close embraces—in a word, such voices of love—as are well understood by those souls whom he loves, and who seek for nothing but himself alone.

(Converse IV)

Lastly, to make a brief summary of what has already been said at large, I will not omit to suggest a devout practice whereby you may fulfil all your daily actions in a manner pleasing to God.

When you wake in the morning, let it be your first thought to raise your mind to him, offering to his glory all that you shall do or suffer that day, praying to him to assist you by his grace. Then make your other morning acts of devotion, acts of thanksgiving and of love, prayers, and resolutions to live that day as though it were to be the last of your life.

(Converse V)

PRAYER

We have already commented on Liguori's *How to Converse Continually . . . with God.* We now focus, in the next selection, on a few pearls of *The Great Means of Salvation and Perfection.* Since my first reading of *The Great Means* many years ago, and I have read it many times since, I have all but memorized the four-page introduction to this great work because I have been charmed at how familiarly Liguori himself is able to converse with his unknown readers. I like to feel the saint used the very same charming and familiar style in praying to God, Jesus and Mary. Because I feel so strongly about the candid familiarity of that introduction, I would consider it presumptuous for me to write my own lead-in for the following selections from *The Great Means* and, therefore, I am inviting you to sit, in spirit, on the other side of Liguori's tiny writing desk and listen to him as he composes his own lead-in. What follows is his own Introduction.

The Great Means of Salvation and Perfection

I do not think I have ever written a book more useful than the present one in which I speak of prayer as a necessary and certain means of obtaining salvation and all the graces we require for that object. If it were in my power, I would distribute a copy of it to every Catholic in the world, in order to show him the necessity of prayer for salvation.

I say this because, on the one hand, I see that its absolute necessity is taught throughout the scriptures and by all the holy Fathers. On the other hand, I see that Christians are very careless in the practice of this great means of salvation. And sadder still, I see that preachers take very little care to speak of it to their flocks, and confessors to their penitents. I see, moreover, that even the spiritual books now popular do not speak sufficiently of it; for there is not a thing preachers and confessors and spiritual books should insist upon with more warmth and energy than prayer. They do, indeed, teach many things which are excellent for keeping ourselves in the grace of God, such as avoiding the occasions of sin, frequenting the sacraments, resisting temptations, hearing God's word and meditating on the eternal truths, and other means—all of them I admit are most useful. However, I say what profit is there in all these sermons, meditations, and all the other means pointed out by the masters of the spiritual life, if we forget to pray, since our Lord has declared he will grant his graces to no one who does not pray. "Ask and you shall receive!"

In the ordinary course of providence, without prayer, all the meditations, all our resolutions, all our promises will be useless. If we do not pray, we shall always be unfaithful to the inspirations of God and to our promises which we have made to him. Why? Because in order to actually do good, to conquer temptations, to practice virtues and to observe God's law, it is not enough to receive illuminations from God, and to meditate and make resolutions; we require, moreover, the actual assistance of God and, as we shall soon see, he does not give his assistance except to those who pray, and pray with perseverance.

My intention in prefacing this work with this sentiment is that my readers may take this opportunity, by means of this little book, to receive

the grace of reflecting more deeply on the importance of prayer; for all
adults who are saved are ordinarily saved by this single means of grace.
And, therefore, I ask my readers to thank God, for it is surely a great mercy
when he gives the light and the grace to pray. . . .

The Apostle writes to Timothy: "I beseech, therefore, that supplica-
tions, petitions, and thanksgivings be made" (1 Tm 2:1). St. Thomas
Aquinas calls prayer the lifting up of the mind and heart to God. Petition
is that kind of prayer which asks for determinate objects. When the thing
asked for is indeterminate we simply say, for example, "Incline unto my
aid, O God," and that is called supplication. Finally, thanksgiving is the
returning of thanks for benefits received, whereby, says Aquinas, we merit
even greater favors. In the strict sense, says Thomas, prayer means having
recourse to God; but in its general sense it includes all the kinds just
mentioned.

(Great Means, Introduction)

Although the first graces that come to us without any cooperation on
our part, such as the call to faith or to penance, are, as St. Augustine says,
granted by God even to those who do not pray; yet the saint considers it
certain that the other graces, and specially the grace of perseverance, are
not granted except in answer to prayer: "God gives us some things, as the
beginning of faith, even when we do not pray. Other things, such as
perseverance, he has only provided for those who pray."

Hence it is that the generality of theologians, following St. Basil, St.
Chrysostom, Clement of Alexandria, St. Augustine, and other Fathers,
teach that prayer is necessary to adults, not only because of the obligation
of the precept (as they say), but because it is necessary as a means of
salvation. That is to say, in the ordinary course of providence, it is
impossible that Christians should be saved without recommending themselves to God, and asking for the graces necessary to salvation. St. Thomas
teaches the same: "After baptism, continual prayer is necessary to us, in
order that we may enter heaven; for though by baptism our sins are
remitted, there still remain concupiscence to assail us from within, and
the world and the devil to assail us from without." The reason then which
makes us certain of the necessity of prayer is shortly this, in order to be
saved we must contend and conquer: "If one takes part in an athletic
contest, he cannot receive the winner's crown unless he has kept the rules"
(2 Tm 2:5). But without the divine assistance we cannot resist the might

of so many and so powerful enemies: now this assistance is only granted to prayer; therefore without prayer there is no salvation.

Moreover, that prayer is the only ordinary means of receiving the divine gifts is more distinctly proved by St. Thomas in another place, where he says, that whatever graces God has from all eternity determined to give us, he will only give them if we pray for them. St. Gregory says the same thing: "By prayer we merit to receive that which God had from all eternity determined to give us." Not, says St. Thomas, that prayer is necessary in order that God may know our necessities, but in order that we may know the necessity of having recourse to God to obtain the help necessary for our salvation, and may thus acknowledge him to be the author of all our good. As, therefore, it is God's law that we should provide ourselves with bread by sowing corn, and with wine by planting vines; so has he ordained that we should receive the graces necessary to salvation by means of prayer: "Ask, and you will receive. Seek, and you will find" (Mt 7:7).

We, in a word, are merely beggars, who have nothing but what God bestows on us as alms: "I am afflicted and poor" (Ps 40:18). The Lord, says St. Augustine, desires and wills to pour forth his graces upon us, but will not give them except to those who pray. "God wishes to give, but only gives to those who ask." This is declared in the words, "Seek, and you will find." Whence it follows, says St. Teresa, that who seeks not, does not receive. As moisture is necessary for the life of plants, to prevent them from drying up, so, says St. Chrysostom, is prayer necessary for our salvation. Or, as he says in another place, prayer vivifies the soul, as the soul vivifies the body: "As the body without the soul cannot live, so the soul without prayer is dead and emits an offensive odor." He uses these words, because people who omit to recommend themselves to God, at once begin to be defiled with sins. Prayer is also called the food of the soul, because the body cannot be supported without food; nor can the soul, says St. Augustine, be kept alive without prayer: "As the flesh is nourished by food, so is the human being supported by prayers." All these comparisons used by the holy Fathers are intended by them to teach the absolute necessity of prayer for the salvation of everyone.

(Great Means I, I, I)

God knows how useful it is to us to be obliged to pray, in order to keep us humble, and to exercise our confidence; and he therefore permits us to be assaulted by enemies too mighty to be overcome by our own strength, that by prayer we may obtain from his mercy aid to resist them; and it is especially to be remarked, that we cannot resist the impure temptations of the flesh, without recommending ourselves to God when we are tempted. This foe is so terrible that, when he fights with us, he, as it were, takes away all light; he makes us forget all our meditations, all our good resolutions; he makes us also disregard the truths of faith, and even almost lose the fear of the divine punishments. For he conspires with our natural inclinations, which drive us with the greatest violence to the indulgence of sensual pleasures. Who in such a moment does not have recourse to God is lost. The only defence against this temptation is prayer, as St. Gregory of Nyssa says: "Prayer is the bulwark of chastity." . . . Chastity is a virtue which we have not strength to practice, unless God gives it us; and God does not give this strength except to who asks for it. But whoever prays for it will certainly obtain it. . . . There is no doubt that we are too weak to resist the attacks of our enemies. But, on the other hand, it is certain that God is faithful, as the apostle says, and will not permit us to be tempted beyond our strength: "God keeps his promise. He will not let you be tested beyond your strength. Along with the test he will give you a way out of it so that you may be able to endure it" (1 Cor 10:13).

(Great Means I, I, II)

But in order to understand better the value of prayers in God's sight, it is sufficient to read both in the Old and New Testaments the innumerable promises which God makes to those who pray. "Call upon me, and I will rescue you" (Ps 50:15). "Call to me, and I will answer you" (Jer 33:3). "Ask, and you will receive. Seek, and you will find. Knock, and it will be opened to you. [He will] give good things to anyone who asks" (Mt 7:7). "Whoever asks, receives; whoever seeks, finds" (Lk 11:10). "You may ask what you will — it will be done for you" (Jn 15:7). "If two of you join your voices on earth to pray for anything whatever, it shall by granted you" (Mt 18:19). "Whatever you ask for in prayer, it shall be done for you" (Mk 11:24). "Anything you ask me in my name, I will do. Whatever you ask the Father, he will give you in my name" (Jn 14:14, 16:23). There are a thousand similar texts; but it would take too long to quote them.

God wills us to be saved; but for our greater good, he wills us to be saved as conquerors. While, therefore, we remain here, we have to live in a continual warfare; and if we should be saved, we have to fight and conquer. "No one can be crowned without victory," says St. Chrysostom.

(Great Means I, II, I)

We are so poor that we have nothing; but if we pray we are no longer poor. If we are poor, God is rich; and God, as the apostle says, is all liberality to who calls for his aid: "Rich in mercy toward all who call upon him" (Rom 10:12). Since, therefore (as St. Augustine exhorts us), we have to do with a Lord of infinite power and infinite riches, let us not go to him for little and valueless things, but let us ask some great thing of him: "You seek from the almighty—seek something great."

There is no doubt that spiritual reading, and meditation on the eternal truths, are very useful things; "but," says St. Augustine, "it is of much more use to pray." By reading and meditating we learn our duty; but by prayer we obtain the grace to do it. "It is better to pray than to read: by reading we know what we ought to do; by prayer we receive what we ask." What is the use of knowing our duty, and then not doing it, but to make us more guilty in God's sight? Read and meditate as we like, we shall never satisfy our obligations, unless we ask of God the grace to fulfil them.

And, therefore, as St. Isidore observes, the devil is never more busy to distract us with the thoughts of worldly cares than when he perceives us praying and asking God for grace: "Then mostly does the devil insinuate thoughts, when he sees a person praying." And why? Because the enemy sees that at no other time do we gain so many treasures of heavenly goods as when we pray.

(Great Means I, II, IV)

The physician who loves his patients will not allow them to have those things that he sees would do them harm. Oh, how many, if they had been sick or poor, would have escaped those sins which they commit in health and in affluence! And, therefore, when people ask God for health or riches, he often denies them because he loves them, knowing that these things would be to them an occasion of losing his grace, or at any rate of growing tepid in the spiritual life. Not that we mean to say that it is any defect to pray to God for the necessaries of this present life, so far as they are not inconsistent with our eternal salvation, as the Wise Man said: "Give me only [what] I need" (Prv 30:8). Nor is it a defect, says St. Thomas, to have anxiety about such goods, if it is not inordinate. The defect consists in desiring and seeking these temporal goods, and in having an inordinate anxiety about them, as if they were our highest good.

It often happens that we pray God to deliver us from some dangerous temptation, and yet that God does not hear us, but permits the temptation to continue troubling us. In such a case, let us understand that God permits even this for our greater good. It is not temptation or bad thoughts that separate us from God, but our consent to the evil. When a soul in temptation recommends itself to God, and by his aid resists, oh, how it then advances in perfection, and unites itself more closely to God! And this is the reason why God does not hear it. St. Paul prayed insistently to be delivered from the temptation of impurity: "I was given a thorn in the flesh, an angel of Satan to beat me. Three times I begged the Lord that this might leave me" (2 Cor 12:7, 8). But God answered him, that it was enough to have his grace: "My grace is enough for you." So that even in temptations we ought to pray with resignation, saying, Lord, deliver me from this trouble, if it is expedient to deliver me; and if not, at least give me help to resist. And here comes in what St. Bernard says, that when we beg any grace of God, he gives us either that which we ask, or some other thing more useful to us.

(Great Means I, III, I)

We ought all to feel that we are standing on the edge of a precipice, suspended over the abyss of all sins, and supported only by the thread of God's grace. If this thread fails us, we shall certainly fall into the gulf, and shall commit the most horrible wickedness. "Were not the Lord my help, I would soon dwell in the silent grave" (Ps 94:17). If God had not succored me, I should have fallen into a thousand sins, and now I should be in hell. So said the psalmist, and so ought each of us to say. This is what St. Francis of Assisi meant, when he said that he was the worst sinner in the world. But, my father, said his companion, what you say is not true; there are many in the world who are certainly worse than you are. Yes, what I say is but too true, answered St. Francis; because if God did not keep his hand over me, I should commit every possible sin.

Hence, whoever has done any good, and has not fallen into greater sins than those which are commonly committed, let him or her say with St. Paul, "By God's favor I am what I am" (1 Cor 15:10); and for the same reason, he ought never to cease to be afraid of falling on every occasion of sin: "Let anyone who thinks he is standing upright watch out lest he fall" (1 Cor 10:12). St. Paul wishes to warn us that who feels secure of not falling, is in great danger of falling; and he assigns the reason in another place, where he says, "If anyone thinks he amounts to something, when in fact he is nothing, he is only deceiving himself" (Gal 6:3).

And so, for like reasons, we should all abstain from noticing with any vainglory the sins of other people; but rather we should then esteem ourselves as worse in ourselves than they are, and should say, Lord, if you had not helped me, I should have done worse. Otherwise, to punish us for our pride, God will permit us to fall into worse and more shameful sins. For this cause St. Paul instructs us to labor for our salvation. But how? Always in fear and trembling: "Work with anxious concern to achieve your salvation" (Phil 2:12). Yes; for those who have a great fear of falling, distrust their own strength, and therefore place their confidence in God, and will have recourse to him in dangers; and God will aid them, and so they will vanquish their temptations, and will be saved. St. Philip Neri, walking one day through Rome, kept saying, "I am in despair!" A certain religious rebuked him, and the saint thereupon said, "My father, I am in despair for myself; but I trust in God."

(Great Means I, III, II)

But on what, a person will say, am I, a miserable sinner, to found this certain confidence of obtaining what I ask? On what? On the promise made by Jesus Christ: "Ask, and you shall receive" (Jn 16:24). "Who will fear to be deceived, when the truth promises?" says St. Augustine. How can we doubt that we shall be heard, when God, who is truth itself, promises to give us that which we ask of him in prayer? "We should not be exhorted to ask," says the same Father, "unless he meant to give." Certainly God would not have exhorted us to ask him for favors, if he had not determined to grant them; but this is the very thing to which he exhorts us so strongly, and which is repeated so often in the scriptures—pray, ask, seek, and you shall obtain what you desire: "You may ask what you will—it will be done for you" (Jn 15:7). And in order that we may pray to him with due confidence, our Savior has taught us, in the Our Father, that when we have recourse to him for the graces necessary to salvation (all of which are included in the petitions of the Lord's Prayer) we should call him, not Lord, but Father—Our Father.

And although sometimes, when we are in a state of aridity, or disturbed by some fault we have committed, we perhaps do not feel while praying that sensible confidence which we would wish to experience, yet, for all this, let us force ourselves to pray, and to pray without ceasing; for God will not neglect to hear us. Nay, rather he will hear us more readily; because we shall then pray with more distrust of ourselves; and confiding only in the goodness and faithfulness of God, who has promised to hear the person who prays to him. Oh, how God is pleased in the time of our tribulations, of our fears, and of our temptations, to see us hope against hope; that is, in spite of the feeling of diffidence which we then experience because of our desolation! This is that for which the apostle praises the patriarch Abraham, who against hope, believed in hope (cf. Rom 4:18).

When we find ourselves weak, and unable to overcome any passion, or any great difficulty, so as to fulfil that which God requires of us, let us take courage and say, with the apostle, "In him who is the source of my strength I have strength for everything" (Phil 4:13). Let us not say, as some do, I cannot; I distrust myself. With our own strength certainly we can do nothing; but with God's help we can do everything. If God said to anyone, Take this mountain on your back, and carry it, for I am helping you, would not the person be a mistrustful fool if he answered, I will not take it; for I have not strength to carry it? And thus, when we know how miserable and weak we are, and when we find ourselves most encompassed with temptations, let us not lose heart; but let us lift up our eyes to God, and say with David, "The Lord is with me to help me, and I shall look down upon my foes" (Ps 118:7). With the help of my Lord, I shall overcome and laugh to scorn all the assaults of my foes. And when we find ourselves in danger of offending God, or in any other critical position, and are too confused to know what is best to be done, let us recommend ourselves to God, saying, "The Lord is my light and my salvation; whom should I fear?" (Ps 27:1). And let us be sure that God will then certainly give us light, and will save us from every evil.

(Great Means I, III, III)

But, till what time have we to pray? Always, says [St. Chrysostom], till we receive favorable sentence of eternal life; that is to say, till our death: "Do not leave off till you receive." And he goes on to say that the person who resolves, I will never leave off praying till I am saved, will most certainly be saved: "If you say, I will not give in till I have received, you will assuredly receive." The apostle writes that many run for the prize, but that he only receives it who runs till he wins: "You know that while all the runners take part in the race, the award goes to one man. In that case, run so as to win!" (1 Cor 9:24). It is not, then, enough for salvation simply to pray; but we must pray always, that we may come to receive the crown which God promises, but promises only to those who are constant in prayer till the end.

(Great Means I, III, IV)

MEDITATIONS

The section of this book you are about to read is entitled, quite simply, *Meditations* (note the plural!). It is just seven little selections of good, solid considerations on various topics, each one of which would, if mulled over properly, lead you into a prayerful response. They are samples of the kind of thought-material that would raise the mind to God and then *per consequens* raise the heart to God. These seven selections are not, therefore, prayers; they are the spiritual spark plugs which ignite real prayer. Let me explain that a bit more.

Alphonsus' understanding of mental prayer was arrived at in the milieu which saw mental prayer as a systematic methodology. This was a development which took place during the fifteenth and sixteenth centuries. New religious institutes no longer had the leisure time for the prayer of the older contemplative and cloistered monastic Orders. Involved in the hustle and bustle of the active apostolate, founders of the active institutes, like Ignatius Loyola, saw the need for some way of keeping their members in close touch with deep prayer and at least a contemplative spirit if not a contemplative lifestyle. This is how the systematic prayer forms of the active institutes began, and this is what Liguori inherited; namely, there was to be a special, limited, and clearly defined time, place, and methodology of prayer, usually several periods a day. The methodology, in terms of raising the mind and heart to God, consisted in various steps or phases:

a. discursus of the mind, a kind of pious reflection and consideration often aided by spiritual reading;
b. affections of the heart; e.g., affections of love, adoration, thanksgiving, petition, and reparation;
c. finally, concrete resolutions and appropriate proposals.

The key word was "system." After Ignatius, others followed suit, making their own methods or adapting that of Loyola.

In view of the seven "meditations" which follow, we note that there is an important distinction that runs through Alphonsian prayer-teaching. He usually distinguishes meditation from actual prayer. What he calls "meditation" would be that necessary preparatory stage (at least in active prayer), that initial input of religious raw material to be mulled over by the mind, with the

77

help of the imagination and the memory. The phrase "spiritual head-trip" aptly suggests that there is something more coming, and that something is affective prayer, the responding of the heart. In his *The Way of Salvation*, Liguori says unequivocally: "The great fruit of meditation is the exercise of prayer." In several of his letters to his Redemptorist confreres, he reminds them that they should be beyond the stage of simple meditation and into the affections and petitions which are the heart of mental prayer. In *The Great Means* this is even more explicitly stated.

> Not just good thoughts, but much more, it is the holy affections of the will that are important, such as acts of humility, trust, detachment, abandonment to the divine will, and above all love, which is what unites us to God.

> (*Great Means* II)

Liguori's Method of Mental Prayer

a. The Time and Place

It can be done almost anywhere—at home, at work, walking, when traveling, etc. Solitude of heart is the essential condition, not necessarily solitude of place. As he himself said: "Deserts and caves are not absolutely necessary." The most suitable time seems to be early morning before one gets wrapped up in the day's affairs or evening time, when the daily chores are over.

b. The Actual Process

1. preparation;
2. meditation;
3. praying, petitions, resolutions, etc.;
4. conclusion.

1. *Preparation*: Like the modern practitioners of "Centering Prayer," Liguori sees position as important. Kneeling is the traditional posture but, he says, any position, sitting, lying down, etc., is acceptable as long as it does not lead to distraction.

Next comes a brief spiritual recollection of oneself best done by the three acts of faith, hope, love, humility, contrition, and a petition for light. The practice of the fixed gaze on the Divine-Within comes in here.

2. *Meditation*: If done privately, this begins with a brief reading (e.g., confer the seven selections below). Scripture should be the primary reading or some spiritual book. Alphonsus points out that St. Teresa used a book for seventeen years. When a group meets for prayer, this reading is done in common.

3. *Praying*: For Alphonsus, the affections are the heart of prayer. In *The Great Means* he writes:

> It should be remembered that the advantage of mental prayer consists not so much in the meditating as in making of affections, petitions, and resolutions. These are the three fruits of meditations. As St. Teresa notes: "The progress of a soul does not consist in thinking much about God, but in loving him ardently, and this love is acquired by resolving to do a great deal for him." The act of love is the great chain, the golden chain that binds us to God.
>
> (*Great Means* II)

Petitions: With Alphonsus, petitionary prayer is primary; we ask for God's graces but most of all we ask continually for an increase of love. Petitioning for material blessings are not excluded, of course, but they must remain secondary and must be made with perfect conformity to God's will.

Resolutions: These begin at the wind-down point of prayer. They should be concrete and particular; e.g., to avoid one's predominant fault this day, to accept contradictions from another, to renew one's vows, to curb a specific appetite, etc.

4. *Conclusion*: The conclusion, for Liguori, consists of three acts; namely, thanksgiving for the lights received, a solid proposal to carry out the resolutions just made, and thirdly, a petition for the grace necessary to be faithful today. Liguori had the habit of adding three brief prayer-acts at this final point: a brief prayer for the conversion of sinners, one for the souls in purgatory, and a quick reminder to Mary to intercede for us, for sinners, and for the souls in purgatory.

I have culled this brief schema on the manner of making mental prayer from *The Great Means*, Part II, pages 229-260 of the paperback Grimm edition. Now that you have digested the methodology, why not try the whole process, using one of the seven selections which immediately follow as your meditation input. Liguori has supplied the holy and wholesome thoughts for your head; your heart will make the appropriate prayer-response.

Meditations and Reflections

Was it ever possible that God, the Creator of all things, should have been pleased to die for the love of his creatures? It is of faith that he has done so. "Christ loved you. He gave himself for us" (Eph 5:2). The earth, the heavens, and all nature, with astonishment beheld Jesus, the only begotten Son of God, the lord of the universe, die of intense pain and anguish, on a disgraceful cross; and why? For the love of humanity. And do people believe this and not love God?

I have believed it, O Jesus! and yet not only have I not loved you, but I have frequently offended you. Pardon me, I beseech you, and remind me continually of the death which you have suffered for me, that I may nevermore offend you, but may always love you.

It was not necessary for humanity's salvation that God should die; one drop of his blood, a single tear, or a prayer would have been sufficient, because being of infinite value, it would have redeemed this or a thousand other worlds.

(Meditation 51)

Days and years pass away, pleasures, honors, and riches pass away, and what will be the end? Death will come and strip us of all, and we shall be buried in the grave to corrupt and molder into dust, deserted and forgotten by all. Alas! how, in the end of our lives, will the remembrance of all we have acquired in this world serve for nothing but to increase our anguish and our uncertainty of salvation!

O death, O death, never depart from before my eyes. O God, enlighten me.

"You have folded up my life, like a weaver" (Is 38:12). How many, in the midst of executing their long-contemplated designs, are overtaken by death and deprived of all things! Ah, with what pain and remorse will the goods of this world be regarded, on the bed of death, by those who have been unduly attached to them! To worldlings who are spiritually blind the goods of this present life appear great; but death will discover what they really are, dust—smoke, and vanity. Before the light of this last lamp all the dazzling grandeur of this world will vanish and disappear. The greatest fortunes, the highest honors, when considered on the bed of death, will lose all their value and splendor. The shade of death will obscure even crowns and scepters.

Grant me, O God! Your holy grace, for this alone is all I desire. I am grieved for having ever despised such a treasure. Jesus, have pity on me. . . .

My dear Redeemer, although I knew that by sinning I should forfeit your friendship, yet did I sin; but I hope for pardon from you who have died to purchase pardon for me. Oh, that I had never offended you, my good God! I behold the love which you have shown me; and this increases my grief for having displeased you who is so good a Father. I love you, O Lord! and will never live without loving you; give me perseverance. Mary, my mother, pray to Jesus for me.

(Meditation 54)

So great was God's love for us that, after having loaded us with gifts and graces, he bestowed upon us his own Son: "God so loved the world that he gave his only Son" (Jn 3:16). For us poor miserable worms of the earth, the eternal Father sent his beloved Son into this world to lead a poor and despised life, and to undergo the most ignominious and bitter death that any mortal on earth had ever suffered, an accumulation of internal as well as eternal torments, such as to cause him to exclaim when dying, "My God, my God, why have you forsaken me?" (Mt 27:46). O eternal God! who but yourself, who is a God of infinite love, could have bestowed upon us a gift of such infinite value? I love you, O infinite goodness! I love you, O infinite love!

"[He] did not spare his own Son but handed him over for the sake of us all" (Rom 8:32). But, O God eternal! consider that this divine Son, whom you doomed to die, is innocent, and has ever been obedient to you in all things. You love him even as yourself, how then can you condemn him to death for the expiation of our sins? The eternal Father replies: "It was precisely because he was my Son, because he was innocent, because he was obedient to me in all things, that it was my will he should lay down his life, in order that you might know the greatness of that love which we both bear toward you."

May all creatures forever praise you, O God! for the excess of bounty through which you have caused your own Son to die for the deliverance of us your servants. For the love of this your Son, have pity on me, pardon me, and save me; and let my salvation be to love you forever, both in this world and in the next.

"But God is rich in mercy; because of his great love for us he brought us to live with Christ" (Eph 2:4-5). Too great, says the apostle, too great has been the love of God toward us. We by sin were dead, and he raised us to life again by the death of his Son. But no, such love was not too great for the infinite bounty of our God. Being infinite in all perfection, he was infinite in love.

But, O Lord! how comes it that after you have shown such love toward people, there are so few who love you? How much do I desire to become one of the number of these few! Hitherto I have not known you, my sovereign good, but have forsaken you; I am sorry for it from the bottom of my heart, and will so love you that, though all should leave you, I will never forsake you, my God, my love, and my all. O Mary! unite me ever more and more to my dearest Savior.

(Meditation 64)

Saint Augustine called the thought of eternity the great thought: *magna cogitatio*. This thought has brought the saints to count all the treasures and greatness of this life as nothing more than straw, dust, smoke, and refuse. This thought has sent many anchorites to hide themselves in deserts and caves, and so many noble youths, and even kings and emperors, to shut themselves up in cloisters. This thought has given courage to so many martyrs to endure the torture of piercing nails and heated irons, and even of being burnt in the fire.

No; we are not created for this earth: the end for which God has placed us in the world is this, that with our good deeds we may inherit eternal life. "Your benefit is sanctification as you tend toward eternal life" (Rom 6:22). And, therefore, St. Eucherius said that the only affair that we should attend to in this life is eternity; that is, that we should win a happy eternity, and escape a miserable one. . . . If assured of this end, we are forever blessed; if we fail of it, we are forever miserable.

Happy who lives ever with eternity in view, with a lively faith that he or she must speedily die and enter upon eternity. "The just man shall live by faith" (Gal 3:11). It is faith that makes the just to live in the sight of God, and which gives light to their souls, by withdrawing them from earthly affections, and placing before their thoughts the eternal blessings which God promises to those that love him.

St. Teresa said that all sins had their origin in a want of faith. Therefore, in order to overcome our passions and temptations, we ought constantly to revive our faith by saying: "I believe the life everlasting." I believe that after this life, which will soon be ended, there is an eternal life, either full of joys, or full of pains, which will befall me, according to my merits or demerits.

St. Augustine also said that a person who believes in eternity, and yet is not converted to God, has either lost his senses or his faith. "O eternity!" (these are his words), "he that meditates upon you, and repents not, either has not faith, or he has not heart." In reference to this, St. John Chrysostom relates that the Gentiles, when they saw Christians sinning, thought them either liars or fools. If you believe not (they said) what you say you believe, you are liars; if you believe in eternity and sin, you are fools. "Woe to sinners who enter upon eternity without having known it, because they would not think upon it!" exclaims St. Caesarius; and then he adds, "But oh, double woe! They enter upon it, and they never come forth."

St. Teresa said constantly to her disciples, "My children, there is one soul, one eternity."

(Reflection 1)

All holiness consists in loving God. The love of God is that infinite treasure in which we gain the friendship of God. God is ready to give this treasure of his holy love, but he wills that we earnestly desire it. Who faintly desires any good thing takes little trouble to gain it. On the other hand, St. Laurence Justinian said that an earnest desire lightens all toil, and gives us strength. And thus, who little desires to advance in divine love, instead of becoming more ardent in the way of perfection, ever becomes more and more lukewarm; and thus is ever in imminent peril of falling headlong down some precipice. And, on the other hand, whoever aspires with fervent desire after perfection, and strengthens oneself daily to advance in its path, little by little, with time will attain it. St. Teresa said, "God never gives many favors, except to those who earnestly desire his love." And again, "God leaves no good desire without its reward."

Good desires must be accompanied by a determined spirit to strengthen ourselves in the attainment of the desired blessing. Many desire perfection, but take no right means to gain it; they want to live in a desert, to accomplish great works of penance and prayer, to endure martyrdom; but such desires are nothing better than mere fancies, which instead of benefiting them, do them great harm. "The sluggard's propensity slays him, for his hands refuse to work" (Prv 21:25). Such persons, feeding themselves upon these fruitless desires, pay no heed to the cure of their defects, the mortification of their appetites, and patience in suffering contempt and crosses. They would do great things, but such as are incompatible with their present condition, and therefore their imperfections increase; in every time of adversity they are agitated, every infirmity makes them impatient; and thus they live imperfect, and imperfect they die.

Resolution, resolution, said St. Teresa: "The devil has no dread of irresolute souls." On the contrary, who resolves to give himself truly to God will overcome even what seemed impossible. A resolved will conquers everything. Let us study to redeem the time that is lost; the time that remains, let us give it all to God. All time that is not devoted to God is lost. Do we not fear lest God should abandon us to our lukewarmness, which may lead us to utter ruin? Let us take courage, and live from this day forth upon the holy maxim, "We must please God even to death." Souls thus resolute are assisted by the Lord to fly in the way of perfection.

(Reflection 5)

Mental prayer is, in the first place, necessary, in order that we may have light to go on the journey to eternity. Eternal truths are spiritual things that are not seen with the eyes of the body, but only by the reflection of the mind. Who does not meditate, does not see them, and thus advances with difficulty along the way of salvation. And, further, those who do not meditate, do not know their own failings, and thus, says St. Bernard, they do not detest them; so, also, they do not see the perils of their state, and therefore do not think of avoiding them. But when we meditate, our failings and perils quickly present themselves; and when we see them we seek to remedy them. St. Bernard said that meditation regulates our affections, directs our actions, and corrects our defects.

St. Catherine of Bologna said, "Meditation is the bond which binds the soul to God; the king brought me into the wine-cellar, he fixed his love upon me." This wine-cellar is meditation, in which the soul becomes so inebriated with divine love that it loses, as it were, its sense for the things of the world; it sees only that which pleases its beloved; it speaks only of the beloved; it would only hear of the beloved; every other discourse wearies and troubles it. In meditation, the soul, retiring to converse alone with God, rests upon itself: "Let him sit alone and in silence, when it is laid upon him" (Lam 3:28). When the soul *sits*—that is, shuts itself up in meditation to consider how worthy is God of love, and how great is the love he bears to it—it thus tastes of God, and fills itself with holy thoughts, and detaches itself from earthly affections, and conceives great desires for becoming holy, and finally resolves to give itself wholly to God. And where but in meditation have the saints made their most generous resolutions, which have lifted them up to the highest point of perfection?

Let us hear what St. John of the Cross said, speaking of mental prayer: "Here we open our heart, here we learn sweet doctrine, and make ourselves wholly to belong to God, reserving nothing, and espousing ourselves to him." And St. Aloysius Gonzaga said that no one will ever attain a high degree of perfection who is not much given to meditation. Let us, then, earnestly apply ourselves to it, and not leave it for any weariness that we may experience; this weariness which we endure for God will be abundantly recompensed by him.

(Reflection 14)

In order to practice mental prayer, or meditation, well, and to make it truly profitable to the soul, we must well ascertain the ends for which we attempt it. First, we must meditate in order to unite ourselves more completely to God. It is not so much good thoughts in the intelligence, as good acts of the will, or holy desires, that unite us to God; and such are the acts that we perform in meditation, acts of humility, confidence, self-sacrifice, resignation, and especially of love and of repentance for our sins. Acts of love, says St. Teresa, are those that keep the soul inflamed with holy love.

Secondly, we must meditate in order to obtain from God, by prayer, the graces that are necessary in order to enable us to advance in the way of salvation, to avoid sin, and to take the means that will lead us to perfection. The best fruit, then, that comes from meditation is the exercise of prayer. Almighty God, ordinarily speaking, does not give grace to any but those who pray. St. Gregory writes, "God desires to be entreated, he desires to be constrained, he desires to be, as it were, conquered by importunity." Observe his words, "to be conquered by importunity." At times, in order to obtain graces of special value, it is not enough simply to pray; we must pray urgently, and, as it were, compel God, by our prayers, to give them. It is true that at all times the Lord is ready to hear us; but at the time of meditation, when we are most truly in converse with God, he is most bountiful in giving us his aid.

Above all, we must apply to meditation, in order to obtain perseverance and the holy love of God. Final perseverance is not a single grace, but a chain of graces, to which must correspond the chain of our prayers; if we cease to pray, God will cease to give us his help, and we shall perish. Who does not practice meditation will find the greatest difficulty in persevering in grace till death. Palafox, in his notes on St. Teresa's letters, writes thus: "How will the Lord give us perseverance, if we do not ask it? And how shall we ask for it without meditation? Without meditation there is no communion with God."

Thus must we be urgent with prayers to obtain from God his holy love. St. Francis de Sales said that all virtues come in union with holy love. "Yet all good things together come to me in her company" (Wis 7:11). Let our prayer for perseverance and love, therefore, be continual; and, in order to pray with greater confidence, let us ever bear in mind the promise made us by Jesus Christ, that whatever we seek from God through the merits of his Son, he will give it to us. Let us, then, pray, and pray always, if we would that God should make us bound in every blessing. . . .

We must apply ourselves to meditation, not for the sake of spiritual consolations, but chiefly in order to learn what is the will of God concerning us. . . . Some persons continue meditation as long as consolations continue; but when these cease, they leave off meditation. It is true that God is accustomed to comfort his beloved souls at the time of meditation, and to give them some foretaste of the delights he prepares in heaven for those who love him. These are things which the lovers of the world do not comprehend; they who have no taste except for earthly delights despise those that are celestial. Oh, if they were wise, how surely would they leave their pleasures to shut themselves in their closets, to speak alone with God! Meditation is nothing more than a converse between the soul and God; the soul pours forth to him its affections, its desires, its fears, its requests, and God speaks to the heart, causing it to know his goodness, and the love which he bears it, and what it must do to please him. "I will lead her into the desert, and speak to her heart" (Hos 2:16).

But these delights are not constant, and, for the most part, holy souls experience much dryness of spirit in meditation. "With dryness and temptations," says St. Teresa, "the Lord makes proof of those who love him." And she adds, "Even if this dryness lasts through life, let not the soul leave off meditation; the time will come when all will be well rewarded." The time of dryness is the time for gaining the greatest rewards; and when we find ourselves apparently without fervor, without good desires, and, as it were, unable to do a good act, let us humble ourselves, and resign ourselves, for this very meditation will be more fruitful than others. It is enough then to say, if we can say nothing more, "O Lord! help me, have mercy on me, abandon me not!" Let us also have recourse to our comforter, the most holy Mary. Happy are those who do not leave off meditation in the hour of desolation. God will make them abound in graces; and therefore let them say:

"O my God, how can I expect to be comforted by you! I, who, until this hour, have deserved to be in hell, forever separated from you, and deprived of the power of loving you any more! I do not therefore grieve, O my God! that you deprive me of your consolations; I do not deserve them; I do not pretend to them. It is enough for me to know that you will never repel a soul that loves you. Deprive me not of the power of loving you, and then do with me what you will. If you will that I continue thus afflicted and desolate even till death, and through all eternity, I am content; it is enough that I can say with truth, 'O my God, I love you, I love you!' Mary, Mother of God, have pity on me!"

(Reflection 15)

THE PASSION OF JESUS

With even the little we know of Alphonsus Liguori from the introduction to this book and from the lead-ins for the various selections, we should almost expect that sooner or later he will ask us to meditate on the passion of Jesus Christ, and so he does. I say this because love, union of wills in self-surrender, and the need to prove that love, all go together in a true love story. "Greater love than this nobody has, than to lay down his life for a friend." Superb psychologist of human nature that he was, Alphonsus begins *The Passion and Death of Jesus Christ* by assuring his reader that "there is nothing more apt to stimulate a Christian to love than the word of God itself" as we see it in holy scripture, and surely the suffering and death of Jesus is one of the most vividly told dramas of the gospel. It is obvious that Liguori has learned the gospel lesson well; namely, that you cannot really appreciate what Paul calls "the excessive love" of God unless you have knelt in the Garden of Gethsemane and stood beneath the cross on Calvary.

But he does not leave things at that. Liguori moves on to make the connection between Christ's suffering and death and our own human sufferings. If suffering and death was Christ's way of proving his and his Father's love for us, then we must at least be open to accept suffering as the proof of our love for him. The divine-human *contra-cambio* comes into play once again. Alphonsus, as usual, begins with the Bible, moves through the sufferings of God's already proven lovers, the saints, and finally leads us to consider our own share in Calvary. Let's look at a few paragraphs of his own introduction to this work.

> This is the reason why I invite you to cast a glance at the passion; for you will find therein all the motives that we can have to hope for eternal life, and motives to love God; and in this our salvation consists.

> All the saints cherished a tender devotion toward Jesus Christ in his passion; this is how they sanctified themselves—by kneeling at the feet of Jesus crucified, by meditating especially on his poverty, his humiliations, his sorrows, and by listening to our Lord from the height of his cross. You may also hope to sanctify yourself if you

continue in like manner to consider what your divine Redeemer has done and suffered for you.

There is a second element in Alphonsus' meditations on the passion of Christ. We do not get too far into the work before we meet a chapter with the title: "The love of Jesus in leaving himself for our food before his death." The proving of his excessive love does not end at Calvary: "Jesus, knowing that his hour was come that he should pass out of this world to the Father, having loved his own who were in the world, he loved them till the end" (Jn 13:1). How? By leaving us his whole self in the eucharistic food of the sacrament of the altar—love continued until the end of time. Now, with the gift of the sacrifice of the Mass, there simply is nothing more that the divine lover could give us to demonstrate his love. This is one of the few works of Liguori which begins with a solemn "Invocation of Jesus and Mary." In that invocation this is what he says:

O Savior of the world, O Lover of souls, O Lord, most lovely of all beings! You by the passion came to win our hearts to yourself by showing us the immense love you bore us in redemption, which has brought us a sea of blessings but which cost you a sea of pains and ignominies. It was principally for this purpose that you instituted the most holy sacrament of the altar, in order that we might have a perpetual memorial of your passion. St. Paul said it well: "Every time, then, you eat this bread and drink this cup, you proclaim the death of the Lord" (1 Cor 11:26).

O my Jesus, I pray you make me always remember your passion, and grant that I, overcome at last by so many devices of your love, may return love for you and, by my poor love, show you some sign of gratitude for your excessive love for me.

And you, O Mary, who had so great a part in the passion of your Son, obtain for me I beg you, the grace to experience a taste of that compassion which you felt at the death of Jesus, and obtain for me a spark of that love which wrought all the martyrdom of your afflicted heart. Amen.

I have quoted Alphonsus at length for there have been those who have misinterpreted his great devotion to the passion of Christ, holding that it was simply the result of a maudlin Italian-Spanish preoccupation with suffering and death, with tears and wailing. It is true that his father, Giuseppe Liguori, did have a special devotion to the passion and that, even as a captain of the Royal Navy, he kept in his cabin lovely statuettes of Christ's agony and crucifixion. It is equally true that Alphonsus himself did paint, both in oil and verbally in his sermons, very moving images of the suffering Jesus, but to conclude that his devotion to the passion was nothing more than a sentimental, pietistic aberration is to grossly ignore the solid theology of redemption, as well as an authentic psychology of sacrificial love, both of which are contained in this and many other of his works.

It is also helpful to recall that when Alphonsus wrote these reflections on the passion of Christ he himself was climbing the hill of his own agony and crucifixion—almost bent in two by his physical ailment of the spine and already practically blind and deaf and, in addition, suffering a personal heartbreak at the threatened dissolution of his Redemptorist congregation. At the age of seventy-seven he was already on Calvary where he remained for another fourteen years. It was surely not a frothy sentimentalism which gave him the courage to write these words as he reflected on the passion of Christ: "Lord, I do not merit consolations; but by your grace, just let me keep loving you and I shall be content to live in this desolation for as long as you wish."

The Passion and Death of Jesus Christ

"See what it is to love." It seems as though our Redeemer from the cross said to us all, "See what it is to love," whenever, in order to avoid something that is troublesome, we abandon works that are pleasing in his sight, or at times even go so far as to renounce his grace and his love. He has loved us even unto death, and came not down from the cross till after having left his life thereon.

(Passion, Reflection XII)

St. Laurence Justinian says that the death of Jesus was the most bitter and painful of all the deaths that human beings ever died; since the Redeemer died upon the cross without any, even the slightest, alleviation: "He was crucified wholly without any alleviation of suffering." In the case of other sufferers, the pain is always mitigated, at all events, by some consoling thought; but the pain and sorrow of Jesus in his sufferings were pure pain, pure sorrow, without mitigation: "The extent of the suffering of Christ appears to us from the purity of its pain and sorrow," says the Angelic Doctor. And hence St. Bernard, when contemplating Jesus dying upon the cross, utters this lamentation: O my Jesus when I behold you upon this tree, I find nothing in you from head to foot but pain and sorrow.

(Passion, Reflection XIII)

God has given us his Son; and why? For love alone. Pilate, for fear of the people gave Jesus up to the Jews: "[He] delivered Jesus up to their wishes" (Lk 23:25). But the eternal Father gave his Son to us for the love which he bore us: "[He] handed him over for the sake of us all" (Rom 8:32). St. Thomas says that "love has the nature of a first gift." When a present is made us, the first gift that we receive is that of the love which the donor offers us in the thing that he or she gives: because, observes the Angelic Doctor, the one and only reason of every voluntary gift is love; otherwise, when a gift is made for some other end than that of simple affection, the gift can no longer rightly be called a true gift. The gift which the eternal Father made us of his Son was a true gift, perfectly voluntary, and without any merit of ours; and therefore it is said that the incarnation of the Word was affected through the operation of the Holy Spirit: that is, through love alone; as the same holy Doctor says: "Through God's supreme love it was brought to pass, that the Son of God assumed to himself flesh."

But not only was it out of pure love that God gave unto us his Son, he also gave him to us with an immensity of love. This is precisely what Jesus wished to signify when he said: "God so loved the world" (Jn 3:16). The word "so" (says St. John Chrysostom) signifies the magnitude of the love wherewith God made us this great gift: "The word 'so' signifies the vehemence of the love." And what greater love could one who was God have been able to give us than was shown by his condemning to death his innocent Son in order to save us miserable sinners? "[He] did not spare his own Son but handed him over for the sake of us all" (Rom 8:32).

Passion, Reflection XV)

"Oh, if you would know the mystery of the cross," said St. Andrew to the tyrant. O tyrant (it was his wish to say), were you to understand the love which Jesus Christ has borne you, in willing to die upon a cross to save you, you would abandon all your possessions and earthly hopes, in order to give yourself wholly to the love of this your Savior. The same ought to be said to those Catholics who, believing as they do, the passion of Jesus, yet do not think of it. Ah, were all people to think upon the love which Jesus Christ has shown forth for us in his death, who would ever be able not to love him? It was for this end, says the apostle, that he, our beloved Redeemer, died for us, that, by the love he displayed toward us in his death, he might become the possessor of our hearts: "That is why Christ died and came to life again, that he might be Lord of both the dead and the living" (Rom 14:9). Whether, then, we die or live, it is but just that we belong wholly to Jesus, who has saved us at so great a cost. Oh, who is there that could say, as did the loving martyr St. Ignatius, whose lot it was to give his life for Jesus Christ, "Let fire, cross, beasts, and torments of every kind come upon me; let me only have fruition of you, O Christ." Let flames, crosses, wild beasts, and every kind of torture come upon me, provided only that I obtain and enjoy my Jesus Christ.

(*Passion,* Reflection XVI)

As Jesus and Barabbas were proposed to the people, so it was proposed to the eternal Father to save his Son or sinful people. The eternal Father answered, Let my Son die, and let sinful people be saved. This the apostle has declared: "[He] did not spare his own Son but handed him over for the sake of us all" (Rom 8:32). The Father would not spare his own Son, but consigned him to death for us all. Yes, said our Savior, God has so loved the world that for its salvation he delivered up his only-begotten Son to torments and death.

(Passion, Exposition VIII)

Behold the unjust sentence of death is read in the presence of our condemned Lord. He listens to it, and, with entire resignation to the just decree of his eternal Father, who condemns him to the cross, he humbly accepts it, not for the crimes falsely imputed to him by the Jews, but in atonement for our real sins, for which he offered to make satisfaction by his death. Pilate says on earth, Let Jesus die. And the eternal Father from heaven confirms the sentence, saying, Let my Son die. The Son himself answers, Here I am; I obey; I accept death, and the death of the cross. "He humbled himself, obediently accepting even death, death on a cross" (Phil 2:8).

(Passion, Exposition XII)

My soul, raise your eyes, and behold that crucified Man-God. Behold that divine lamb sacrificed on that altar of pain; consider that he is the beloved Son of the eternal Father, and consider he has died through the love he has borne you. See how his arms are stretched out to embrace you; his head bowed down to give you the kiss of peace; his side opened to receive you. What do you say? Does a God so good and so loving deserve to be loved? Listen to what the Lord says to you from the cross: My Son, see if there is any one in this world who has loved you more than I, your God, have loved you.

Ah, my God and my Redeemer, you, then, have died, and died the most infamous and painful death. And why? To gain my love.

(Passion, Exposition XVI)

When the divine Word offered himself to redeem humankind, there were before him two ways of redemption, the one of joy and glory, the other of pains and insults. At the same time, it was his will, not only by his coming to deliver humanity from eternal death, but also to call forth the love of all the hearts of people, and therefore he rejected the way of joy and glory, and chose that of pains and insults: "For the sake of the joy which lay before him he endured the cross" (Heb 12:2). In order that he might satisfy the divine justice for us, and, at the same time, inflame us with his holy love, he was willing to endure this burden of all our sins; that, dying upon a cross, he might obtain for us grace and the life of the blessed. This is what Isaiah intended to express when he said: "Yet it was our infirmities that he bore, our sufferings that he endured" (Is 53:4).

Of this there were two express figures in the Old Testament; the first was the annual ceremony of the scapegoat, which the high-priest represented as bearing all the sins of the people, and therefore all, loading it with curses, drove it into the desert, to be the object of the wrath of God. This goat was a figure of our Redeemer, who was willing to load himself with all the curses deserved by us for our sins; being made a curse for us, in order that he might obtain for us the divine blessing. Therefore the apostle wrote in another place, "For our sakes God made him who did not know sin, to be sin, so that in him we might become the very holiness of God" (2 Cor 5:21). That is, as St. Ambrose and St. Anselm explain it, he made him to be sin who was innocence itself; that is, he presented himself to God as if he had been sin itself. In a word, he took upon himself the character of a sinner, and endured the pains due to us sinners, in order to render us just before God.

And Jesus accepted such a death. He died to pay the price of our sins; and therefore, as a sinner, he desired to be circumcised; to be redeemed with a price when he was presented in the temple; to receive the baptism of repentance from the Baptist; and lastly, in his passion, to be nailed upon the cross to atone for our guilty wanderings: to atone for our avarice, by being stripped of his garments; for our pride, by the insults he endured; for our desires of power, by submitting himself to the executioner; for our evil thoughts, by his crown of thorns; for our intemperance, by the gall he tasted; and by the pangs of his body, for our sensual delights.

Hence St. Paul says, "No, I determined that while I was with you I would speak of nothing but Jesus Christ and him crucified" (1 Cor 2:2). The apostle well knew that Jesus Christ was born in a cave; that, for thirty years, he inhabited a carpenter's shop; that he had risen from the dead, and had ascended into heaven. Why, then, did he say that he would speak of nothing but Jesus crucified? Because the death suffered by Jesus Christ on the cross was that which most moved him to love him, and induced him to exercise obedience toward God and love toward his neighbor, which were the virtues most specially inculcated by Jesus Christ from the chair of his cross. St. Thomas, the Angelic Doctor, writes: "in whatever temptation we fall, in the cross is our protection; there is obedience to God, love to our neighbor, patience in adversity; when St. Augustine says, 'The cross was not only the instrument of death to the sufferer, but his chair of teaching.' "

(Passion, Consideration I)

To form a conception of what Jesus Christ suffered in his life, and still more in his death, we must consider what the same apostle says in his letter to the Romans: "God sent his Son in the likeness of sinful flesh as a sin offering, thereby condemning sin in the flesh" (Rom 8:3). Jesus Christ being sent by the Father to redeem humanity clothed himself with that flesh which was infected with sin; and though he had not contracted the pollution of sin, nevertheless he took upon him the miseries contracted by human nature, as the punishment of sin; and he offered himself to the eternal Father, to satisfy the divine justice for all the sins of humanity by his sufferings; he was offered because he himself willed it; and the eternal Father, as Isaiah writes, "laid upon him the guilt of us all" (Is 53:6). Behold Jesus, therefore, laden with all the blasphemies, all the sacrileges, trespasses, thefts, cruelties, and abominable deeds which people have committed and will commit. Behold him, in a word, the object of all the divine curses which people have deserved through their sins: "Christ has delivered us from the power of the law's curse by himself becoming a curse for us" (Gal 3:13).

Therefore St. Thomas writes that both the internal and outward pains of Jesus Christ exceeded all the pains which can be endured in this life.

And thus Jesus voluntarily, through his own goodness, making himself the debtor for our debts, chose to sacrifice himself altogether, even to death in the pains of the cross, as he himself says in the Gospel of St. John: "That I lay down my life to take it up again. No one takes it from me; I lay it down freely" (Jn 10:17, 18).

(Passion, Consideration II)

Finally, to speak of all alike, both the just and sinners, everyone has his own cross. The just, though they enjoy peace of conscience, yet all have their vicissitudes; at one time they are comforted by visits of divine mercy, at another they are afflicted by bodily vexations and infirmities, and especially by desolation of spirit, by darkness and weariness, by scruples and temptations, and by fears for their own salvation. Much heavier are the crosses of sinners, through remorse of conscience, through the terrors of eternal punishment, which from time to time affright them, and through the pains they suffer when things go wrong with them. The saints, when adversities befall them, unite themselves with the divine will, and suffer them with patience; but how can sinners calm themselves by recollecting the divine will, when they are living at enmity with God? The pains of the enemies of God are unmixed pains, pains without relief. Wherefore St. Teresa was wont to say "who loves God embraces the cross, and thus does not feel it; while who does not love him drags the cross along by force and thus cannot but feel it."

Jesus upon the cross was a spectacle which filled heaven and earth with amazement, at the sight of an almighty God, the Lord of all, dying upon an infamous gibbet condemned as a malefactor between two other malefactors. It was a spectacle of justice, in displaying the eternal Father, in order that his justice might be satisfied; punishing the sins of humanity in the person of his only begotten Son, loved by him as himself. It was a spectacle of mercy, displaying his innocent Son dying a death so shameful and so bitter, in order to save his creatures from the punishment that was due to them. Especially was it a sight of love, in displaying a God who offered and gave his life to redeem from death his slaves and enemies.

It is this spectacle which ever was and ever will be the dearest object of the contemplation of the saints, through which they have counted it little to strip themselves of all earthly pleasures and goods, and to embrace with desire and joy both pain and death, in order to make some return of gratitude to a God who died for love of them.

(Passion, Consideration III)

They said, "Save yourself." O ungrateful people! If this great Son of God, when he was made man, had chosen to save himself, he would not voluntarily have chosen death.

"If you are the Son of God, come down from the cross" (Mt 27:40); yet, if Jesus had come down, he would not have accomplished our redemption by his death; we could not have been delivered from eternal death. "He would not come down," says St. Ambrose, "lest when he came down, I should die."

(Passion, Consideration IV)

The afflicted mother thus was standing close to the cross; and as the Son sacrificed his life, so she offered her pangs for the salvation of humanity sharing with perfect resignation all the pains and insults which her Son suffered in his death. A writer says that they who would describe her fainting at the foot of the cross dishonor the constancy of Mary. She was the strong woman, who neither fainted nor wept, as St. Ambrose writes: "I read of her standing, but not of her weeping."

The pain which the Holy Virgin endured in the passion of her Son exceeded all the pains which a human heart can endure; but the grief of Mary was not a barren grief, like that of other mothers who behold the sufferings of their children; it was a fruitful grief, since through the merits of her so great grief, and through her love (according to the opinion of St. Augustine), as she was the natural mother of our head Jesus Christ, so she then became the spiritual mother of us who are his faithful members, in co-operating with him by her love in causing us to be born, and to be the children of the Church.

God said to the serpent, "I will put enmities between you and the woman" (Gn 3:15). This shows that after the fall of humanity through sin, notwithstanding all that would be done by the redemption of Jesus Christ, there would be two families and two posterities in the world, the seed of Satan signifying the family of sinners, his children corrupted by him, and the seed of Mary signifying the holy family, which includes all the just, with their head Jesus Christ. Hence Mary was destined to be the mother both of the head and of the members, namely the faithful. The apostle writes: "All are one in Christ Jesus. Furthermore, if you belong to Christ you are the descendants of Abraham" (Gal 3:28, 29). Thus Jesus Christ and the faithful are one single body, because the head cannot be divided from the members, and these members are all spiritual children of Mary, as they have the same spirit of her Son according to nature, who was Jesus Christ. Therefore, St. John was not called *John,* but the disciple beloved by the Lord, that we might understand that Mary is the mother of every good Christian who is beloved by Jesus Christ, and in whom Jesus Christ lives by his Spirit. This was expressed by Origen, when he said, "Jesus said to Mary, Behold your son, as if he had said, This is Jesus, whom you have borne, for he who is perfected lives no more himself, but Christ lives in him."

St. Leo writes that this cry of the Lord was not a lamentation, but a doctrine, because he thus desired to teach us how great is the wickedness of sin, which, as it were, compelled God to abandon his beloved Son without a comfort, because he had taken upon him to make satisfaction for our sins. At the same time, Jesus was not abandoned by the divinity, nor deprived of the glory which had been communicated to his blessed soul from the first moment of his creation; but he was deprived of all that sensible relief by which God is wont to comfort his faithful servants in their sufferings; and he was left in darkness, fear, and bitterness, pangs which were deserved by us. This deprivation of the sensible consciousness of the divine presence was also endured by Jesus in the Garden of Gethsemane; but that which he suffered on the cross was greater and more bitter.

O Eternal Father, what offence had this your innocent and most obedient Son ever given you, that you should punish him with a death so bitter? Look at him as he hangs upon this cross, with his head tortured with thorns, as he hangs upon the three iron nails, and is supported by his own wounds! All have abandoned him, even his own disciples, all deride him upon the cross, and blaspheme him; and why have you abandoned him, who have so greatly loved him? We must understand that Jesus had taken upon himself the sins of the world, although he was himself the most holy of all beings, and even sanctity itself; since he had taken upon himself to satisfy for all our sins, he seemed the greatest of all sinners; and having thus made himself guilty for all, he offered himself to pay the price for all. Because we had deserved to be abandoned forever in hell to eternal despair, therefore he chose to be given up to death deprived of every relief, that thus he might deliver us from eternal death.

Therefore, let us give thanks to the goodness of our Savior for having been willing to take upon himself the pains which were due to us, and thus to deliver us from eternal death; and let us labor henceforth to be grateful to this our deliverer, banishing from our hearts every affection which is not for him. And when we find ourselves desolate in spirit, and deprived of the sense of the divine presence, let us unite our desolation to that which Jesus Christ suffered in his death. Sometimes he hides himself from the souls that he most loves, but he does not really leave their hearts; he aids them with his inward grace. He is not offended, if in such an abandonment we say, as he himself said in the garden to his divine Father, "My Father, if it is possible, let this cup pass me by" (Mt 26:39). But at the same time we must add, "Still, let it be as you would have it, not as I" (Mt 26:39). And if the desolation continues, we must continue the same acts of conformity to the divine will, as he himself repeated them for the three hours during which he prayed in the garden. St. Francis de Sales says that Jesus is as worthy of love when he hides himself as when he makes himself seen. Further, who has deserved hell, and finds himself out of it, should say only, "I will bless the Lord at all times" (Ps 34:2). O Lord, I do not deserve consolations; grant that through your grace I may love you, and I am content to live in desolation as long as it pleases you.

(*Passion,* Consideration V)

To obtain perseverance in good, we must not trust in our resolutions and in the promises we have made to God; if we trust in our own strength, we are lost. All our hope of preserving the grace of God must be placed in the merits of Jesus Christ, and thus, trusting in his help, we shall persevere till death, though we were attacked by all our enemies in earth and hell. Sometimes we find ourselves so cast down in mind, and so assaulted by temptations, that we seem almost lost; let us not then lose courage, nor abandon ourselves to despair; let us go to the Crucified, and he will hold us up.

The Lord permits his saints sometimes to find themselves in tempests and fears. St. Paul says that the afflictions and terrors which he suffered in Asia were so overpowering that he became weary of life; meaning that he was so, so far as he depended on his own strength, in order to teach us that God, from time to time, leaves us in desolations, in order that we may know our misery, and, distrusting ourselves, may humbly have recourse to his goodness, and gain from him strength not to fall. More clearly he expresses the same in another place, "We are afflicted in every way possible, but we are not crushed" (2 Cor 4:8). We find ourselves oppressed with sadness and passions, but do not abandon ourselves to despair; we are tossed about on the water, but do not sink, because the Lord, by his grace, gives us strength against our enemies. But the apostle exhorts us ever to bear before our eyes that we are weak, and prone to lose the treasure of divine grace, and that all our strength for preserving it comes not from ourselves but from God: "This treasure we possess in earthen vessels, to make it clear that its surpassing power comes from God and not from us" (2 Cor 4:7).

Let us, then, be firmly persuaded that in this life we must ever beware of placing any confidence in our own works. Our strongest armor with which we shall ever win the victory over the assaults of hell is prayer. This is the armor of God of which St. Paul speaks: "Put on the armor of God so that you may be able to stand firm against the tactics of the devil. Our battle is not against human forces but against the principalities and powers, the rulers of this world of darkness, the evil spirits in regions above. You must put on the armor of God if you are to resist on the evil day; do all that your duty requires, and hold your ground. Stand fast, with the truth as the belt around your waist, justice as your breastplate, and zeal to propagate the gospel of peace as your footgear. In all circumstances hold faith up before you as your shield; it will help you extinguish the fiery darts of the evil one. Take the helmet of salvation and the sword of the spirit, the word of God" (Eph 6:11-17).

Let us pause and weigh well these various expressions. "Stand fast with the truth as the belt around your waist." There the apostle alludes to the military girdle with which soldiers gird themselves as a token of the fidelity which they have sworn to their sovereign. The girdle which the Christian must put on is the possession of the truth of the doctrine of Jesus Christ, in accordance with which we must repress all inordinate passions, especially those of impurity, which are the most dangerous of all.

"Justice as your breastplate." The Christian's breastplate is a good life, without which he will have little strength to resist the assaults of his foes.

"And zeal to propagate the gospel of peace as your footgear." The military shoes which the Christian ought to wear, in order that he or she may go speedily where it is necessary, unlike those whose feet are bare, and who walk slowly, is the possession of a mind prepared to embrace in practice, and to teach by example, the holy maxims of the gospel.

"In all circumstances hold faith up before you as your shield." The shield with which the soldier of Christ must defend himself against the fiery darts (that is, darts which pierce like fire) of the enemy is a steady faith, strengthened with holy hope, and especially with divine charity. "Take the helmet of salvation and the sword of the spirit." The helmet, as St. Anselm teaches us, is the hope of eternal salvation; and, lastly, the sword of the Spirit, our spiritual sword, is the divine word, by which God repeatedly promises to hear those who pray to him. "Seek, and you will find" (Mt 7:7). "Whoever seeks, finds" (Lk 11:10). "Call to me and I will answer you" (Jer 33:3). "Then call upon me in time of distress; I will rescue you" (Ps 49:15). "At every opportunity pray in the Spirit, using prayers and petitions of every sort. Pray constantly and attentively for all in the holy company" (Eph 6:18). Thus, prayer is the most powerful of the arms with which the Lord gives us victory over our evil passions and the temptations of hell; but this prayer must be made *in the spirit*; that is, not with the mouth only, but with the heart. Moreover, it must last through our life — "at all times;" for as the struggle endures, so must our prayers. It must be urgent and repeated; if the temptation does not yield at the first prayer, we must repeat it a second, third, or fourth time; and if it still continues, we must add sighs, tears, importunity, vehemence, as if we would do violence to God, that he may give us the grace of victory. This is what the apostle's words, "with all instance and supplication," mean. The apostle adds, "for all saints," which means that we are not to pray for ourselves alone; but for the perseverance of all the faithful who are in the grace of God, and especially of priests, that they may labor for the conversion of unbelievers and all sinners, repeating in our prayers the words of Zechariah, "To shine on those who sit in darkness and in the shadow of death" (Lk 1:79).

It is of great use for resisting our enemies in spiritual combats, to anticipate them in our meditations, by preparing ourselves to do violence to them to our utmost power, on all occasions when they may suddenly come upon us. Thus the saints have been able to preserve the greatest mildness, or at least not to reply by a single word, and not to be disturbed when they have received a great injury, a violent persecution, a severe pang in body or in mind, the loss of property of great value, the death of a much-loved relative. Such victories are ordinarily not acquired without the aid of a life of long discipline, without frequenting sacraments, and a continual exercise of meditation, spiritual reading, and prayer. Therefore these victories are with difficulty obtained by those who have not taken great heed to avoid dangerous occasions, or who are attached to the vanities or pleasures of the world, and practice very little the mortification of the senses; by those, in a word, who live a soft and easy life. St. Augustine says that in the spiritual life, "first, pleasures are to be conquered, then pains"; meaning that a person who is given to seek the pleasures of the senses will scarcely resist a great passion or temptation which assails him or her; a person who loves too much the esteem of the world will scarcely endure a grave affront without losing the grace of God.

It is true that we must look for all our strength to live without sin, and to do good works, not from ourselves, but from the grace of Jesus Christ; but we must take great care not to make ourselves weaker than we are by nature through our own fault. The defects of which we take no account will cause the divine light to fail, and the devil will become stronger against us. For example, a desire to display to the world our learning, rank, or vanity in dress, or the seeking of any superfluous pleasure, or resentment at every inattentive word or action, or a wish to please everyone, though at the loss of our spiritual profit, or neglect of works of piety through the fear of people or little acts of disobedience toward our superiors, little murmurings, trifling but cherished aversions, trivial falsehoods, slight attacks upon our neighbor, loss of time in gossip, or the indulgence of curiosity—in a word, every attachment to earthly things, and every act of inordinate self-love, can serve as a help to our enemy to drag us over some precipice; or, at least, this defect deliberately consented to will deprive us of that abundance of divine help without which we may find ourselves fallen into ruin.

(Passion, Consideration X)

To speak of patience and suffering is a thing neither practiced nor understood by those who love the world. It is understood and practiced only by souls who love God. "O Lord," said St. John of the Cross to Jesus Christ, "I ask nothing of you but to suffer and to be despised for your sake." St. Teresa frequently exclaimed, "O my Jesus, I would either suffer or die." St. Mary Magdalene of Pazzi was wont to say, "I would suffer and not die." Thus speak the saints who love God, because a soul can give no surer mark to God of love for him than voluntarily to suffer to please him.

Thomas à Kempis writes, "The cross everywhere awaits you; it is needful for you everywhere to preserve patience, if you want to have peace. If you willingly bear the cross, it will bear you to your desired end." In this world, we all go about seeking peace; and would want to find it without suffering; but this is not possible in our present state; we must suffer; the cross awaits us wherever we turn. How, then, can we find peace in the midst of these crosses? By patience, by embracing the cross, which presents itself to us. St. Teresa says that "who drags the cross along with ill-will feels its weight, however small it is; but who willingly embraces it, however great it is, does not feel it."

The same Thomas à Kempis says, "Which of the saints is without a cross? The whole life of Christ was a cross and a martyrdom, and do you seek for pleasure?" Jesus, innocent, holy, and the Son of God, was willing to suffer through his whole life, and shall we go about seeking pleasures and comforts? To give us an example of patience he chose a life full of ignominies and pains within and without; and shall we wish to be saved without suffering, or to suffer without fruit, and with increase of pain? How can we think to be lovers of Jesus Christ, if we will not suffer for love of him who has so much suffered for love of us? How can those glory in being followers of the Crucified who refuse or receive with ill-will the fruits of the cross, which are sufferings, contempt, poverty, pains, infirmities, and all things that are contrary to our self-love?

Thus the apostle goes on to encourage us, saying, "In your fight against sin you have not yet resisted to the point of shedding blood" (Heb 12:4). Think, he says, that Christ poured forth for you all his blood in his passion through torments, and that the holy martyrs, after the example of him, their king, have courageously endured hot plates, and iron nails, which have torn open their very bowels; but you have not shed a single drop of blood for Jesus Christ, while we ought to be ready to give our life rather than offend God, as St. Oddment said, "I would rather leap into a burning pile than commit a sin against my God." And thus St. Anselm, Archbishop of Canterbury, said, "If I must either endure all the bodily pains of hell, or else commit a sin, rather than commit it I would choose hell."

The infernal lion ceases not through all our life to go about seeking to devour us; therefore St. Peter tells us that, by thinking of the passion of Christ, we ought to arm ourselves against his attacks. St. Thomas says that the mere recollection of the passion is a great defence against all the temptations of hell. And St. Ambrose, or some other saint, says, "If there had been any better way of salvation for people than the way of suffering, Christ would have shown it to us both by word and example."

Let us, then, give ourselves, O souls that love the Crucified, for the life that remains to us, to love this loving Redeemer, so worthy of love, to our utmost power; and also to suffer for him, because he has been willing to suffer for love of us; and let us not cease to ask him continually to grant us the gift of his holy love.

(*Passion,* Consideration XI)

Whilst hanging on the cross, Jesus has no one who can console him. Among those who stand around him, some are blaspheming, some are deriding him; some say, "Come down off the cross if you are God's Son" (Mt 27:42). And he receives no compassion even from those who are his very companions in punishment; nay, rather, one of them joins those others in blaspheming him: "One of the criminals hanging in crucifixion blasphemed him" (Lk 23:39). There stood, it is true, below the cross, Mary assisting with love her dying Son. But the sight of this mother in her sorrows, so far from consoling Jesus, afflicted him so much the more, at seeing the pain which she endured for love of him. So, then, our Redeemer, finding no comfort here on earth, turned himself to the eternal Father in heaven above. But the Father, seeing him covered with all the sins of humankind, for which he was making satisfaction, said, No, my son, I cannot console you. It is meet that even I too should abandon you to your pains, and leave you to die without comfort. And then it was that Jesus cried out, "My God, my God, why have you forsaken me?" (Mt 27:46).

The Redeemer, now nigh to expiring, with dying breath said, "Now it is finished" (Jn 19:30). As if he had said, O humans, all has been completed and done for your redemption. Love me, then, since I have nothing more that I can do to make you love me.

(Passion, Meditations)

THE PREPARATION FOR DEATH

I once heard a claim that the works of St. Alphonsus, especially *The Practice of the Love of Jesus Christ* and *The Preparation for Death,* had a profound influence on Soren Kierkegaard, the granddaddy of modern existential philosophy. The latter's book, *The Works of Love,* surely does bear an uncanny resemblance to Liguori's *The Practice of the Love of Jesus Christ;* both books are a commentary on St. Paul's panegyric to love. Perhaps an even greater influence can be detected in the similarities between Alphonsus' and Soren's thinking on the meaning of Christian death. It is an historical fact that among the few books in the monk-like room of Kierkegaard when he died was *The Preparation for Death,* the very book from which we now present our selection. This fact certainly opens the door to a deeper understanding of the Scandinavian philosopher-theologian and the death-theme that runs through many of his works. Remember, however, that the two men were separated by almost one hundred years. Kierkegaard would have been reading a German translation of *The Preparation for Death.* It seems to me that this work of Liguori would go a long way in alleviating much of the existential *angst* over death and dying that is part of our contemporary world.

The works of Kubler-Ross have made the topic of dying a cocktail party topic. Moreover, the growing presence of death-dealing catastrophes like massive human violence, hunger, war, and, most recently, the worldwide AIDS epidemic have literally brought death and dying to our front doorsteps.

One undeniable reaction to the undeniable reality of death is fear and denial, perhaps even more common today than in the past. Modern medicine, though it has indeed prolonged the human lifespan, at least in the so-called "First World" countries, has at the same time become a kind of new savior from death because of an underlying assumption that no one should die.

Instead of fear and dread, this work of Alphonsus ushers in love and confidence. In the introduction, which he simply calls "The Aim of This Work," it is obvious that he wrote the book in response to a double request: One came from the general public, who wanted to know something on how to live a virtuous life and advance in holiness, the other came from the clergy, who were in search of solid material for retreats and missions. Not to multiply books, labor, and expense, he came up with the idea of this work, since to live this life in a holy way one ought to live it in the light of one's death and the future life. Liguori says that as an aid to the laity, he has divided each meditation into three points followed by concrete affections and other appropriate prayers.

In the light of everything you have read so far in this briefest book of Alphonsian selections, you should be able to guess what the two most essential graces necessary for a holy life and a happy death are. He writes:

> I entreat the reader not to grow weary, if, in these prayers, they always find petitions for *divine love* and for *the grace of perseverance*. For us, these are the two most necessary graces for the attainment of eternal salvation. The grace of divine love contains in itself all other graces because love of God brings with it all other virtues. The grace of perseverance is that grace by which we obtain the eternal crown. However, it is a grace given only to those who ask for it, hence the necessity of a prayerful life as I have demonstrated elsewhere.
>
> I pray my reader to recommend me to Jesus Christ whether I am living or dead when you read this, and I promise to do the same for all who perform this act of charity for me.

The Preparation for Death is truly the final Liguorian word on the so-called *Eternal Truths* which were so precious to Alphonsus. It is true that thoughts on the meaning of life in view of one's death and judgement and on the two final options, heaven and hell, are scattered throughout all of his ascetical works, but this one is the eschatological masterpiece. For Liguori, love is always eschatological because it is meant to be the *élan vital* of our whole life as we move on toward death, which for Alphonsus is not a fearful thing for those who love God. Death itself is, for them, both a final and complete healing of the imperfection of human love and its eternal perfection in heaven.

Before you attempt to read the entire *Preparation for Death,* from which we have selected but one sample, we might take to heart the gentle warning of Albino Cardinal Luciani, whom we have already quoted elsewhere:

> To make sure that he would be understood even by the simplest of his listeners and readers, Alphonsus made us simple, familiar

metaphors — a pedagogical method as old as communication itself — and ever-timely at that! In fact, he proved to be the master of the apt image and illustration and his ascetical writings in particular abound in helpful imagery. I will give you an example . . . from the first point of his Second Consideration in *The Preparation for Death*.

There are two pages in which Alphonsus aims to reach his reader's heart and move his will with the following idea: "Death reaches out for everybody." He then adduces two scripture texts: Ezekiel 7:2, i.e., the end is coming, and James 4:5, i.e., life is like a mist that lingers but for a brief time. He then quotes St. Basil, who searches through a cemetery to see if he can tell who was a servant and who a master. Then he brings in Seneca's statement that we are born unequal but we all die on an equal footing. But then Liguori includes three graphic illustrations of his own:

1. The story of the man who accuses Thomas à Kempis' brother of building a faulty house. Faulty? Why so? Because it has a door and someday they will carry you out of that door dead, and all that beautiful house will have to be left behind.

2. Saladan, an Asian potentate, who ordered that, in his funeral procession, a slave should precede his dead body with a pole with his shirt hanging on it while crying out: Look, this is all that Saladin carries to his grave.

3. Diogenes diligently searching through a pile of skulls. Alexander asks him: "What are you looking for?" Diogenes replied: "I am looking for the skull of your father, Philip, and I cannot tell Philip's from any other. If you can, let me know."

(Pastoral Letter to Clergy of Venice)

The Cardinal's point is well-taken: The message has perennial wisdom and value, the stories, perhaps, more apt for an earlier and simpler age. Read on, however! There are no stories in our selection.

Considerations on the Eternal Truths

What is your life? It is like a vapor, which is dissipated by a blast of wind, and is seen no more. All know that they must die; but the delusion of many is, that they imagine death as far off as if it were never to arrive. But Job tells us that our life is short. "Man born of woman is short-lived and full of trouble, like a flower that springs up and fades" (Jb 14:1, 2). This truth the Lord commanded Isaiah to preach to the people. "Cry out! All mankind is grass. The grass withers, the flower wilts" (Is 40:6). Human life is like the life of a blade of grass; death comes, the grass is dried up: behold, life ends, and the flower of all greatness and of all worldly goods falls off.

"My days," says Job, "are swifter than a runner" (Jb 9:25). Death comes to meet us more swiftly than a runner, and we at every moment run toward death. Every step, every breath brings us nearer to our end. "What I write," says Jerome, "is so much taken away from life." "During the time I write, I draw near to death." . . . Behold how the stream flows to the sea, and the passing waters never return! Thus, my brother, your days pass by, and you approach death. Pleasures, amusements, pomps, praises, and acclamations pass away; and what remains? Only the grave remains for me (cf. Jb 17:1). We shall be thrown into a grave, and there we shall remain to rot, stripped of all things. At the hour of death the remembrance of the delights enjoyed, and of all the honors acquired in this life, will serve only to increase our pain and our diffidence of obtaining eternal salvation. Then the miserable worldling will say: "My house, my gardens, my fashionable furniture, my pictures, my garments, will in a little time be no longer mine, 'and only the grave remains for me.' "

Ah! at that hour all earthly goods are viewed only with pain by those who have had an attachment for them. And this pain will serve only to increase the danger of their eternal salvation; for we see by experience, that persons attached to the world wish at death to speak only of their sickness, of the physicians to be called to attend them, and of the remedies which may restore their health. When any one speaks of the state of the soul, they soon grow weary, and beg to be allowed repose. They complain of headache, and say that it pains them to hear anyone speak. And if they sometimes answer, they are confused, and know not what to say. It often happens that the confessor gives them absolution, not because he knows that they are disposed for the sacrament, but because it is dangerous to defer it. Such is the death of those who think but little of death.

(Preparation III)

What folly would it not be for travellers, who would think only of acquiring dignities and possessions in the countries through which they had to pass, and should reduce themselves to the necessity of living miserably in their native lands, where they must remain during their whole lives! And are not they fools who seek after happiness in this world, where they will remain only a few days, and expose themselves to the risk of being unhappy in the next, where they must live for eternity? We do not fix our affections on borrowed goods, because we know that they must soon be returned to the owner. All the goods of this earth are lent to us: it is folly to set our heart on what we must soon quit. Death shall strip us of them all. The acquisitions and fortunes of this world all terminate in a dying gasp, in a funeral, in a descent into the grave. The house which you have built for yourself you must soon give up to others. The grave will be the dwelling of your body till the day of judgment; thence it will go to heaven or to hell, whither the soul will have gone before.

(Preparation IV)

All know that they must die: but the misfortune is, that many view death at such a distance, that they lose sight of it. Even the old, the most decrepit, and the most sickly, flatter themselves that they will live three or four years longer. But how many, I ask, have we known, even in our own times, to die suddenly — some sitting, some walking, some sleeping? It is certain that not one of these imagined that he or she should die so suddenly, and on that day on which he or she died. I say, moreover, that those who have gone to the other world during the present year, did not imagine that they should die and end their days this year. Few are the deaths which do not happen unexpectedly.

(Preparation V)

Dying persons who have neglected the salvation of their souls, will find thorns in everything that is presented to them—thorns in the remembrance of past amusements, rivalries overcome and pomps displayed; thorns in the friends who will come to visit, and in whatever these friends' presence shall bring before their minds; thorns in the spiritual fathers who assist them in turn; thorns in the sacraments of penance, eucharist, and extreme unction, which they must receive; thorns even in the crucifix which is placed before them. In that sacred image they will read their want of correspondence to the love of a God who died for their salvation.

O fool that I have been! the poor sick person will say, with the lights and opportunities that God has given me, I could have become a saint. I could have led a life of happiness in the grace of God; and after so many years that he gave me, what do I find but torments, distrust, fears, remorse of conscience and accounts to render to God? I shall scarcely save my soul. And when will he say this? When the oil in the lamp is on the point of being consumed, and the scene of this world is about to close forever; when he finds himself in view of two eternities, one happy, the other miserable; when he is near that last gasp on which depends his everlasting bliss or eternal despair, as long as God shall be God.

(Preparation VII)

The just person is not afflicted at the thought of being obliged to take leave of the goods of the earth, for he has always kept his heart detached from them. During life he has constantly said to the Lord: "God is the rock of my heart and my portion forever" (Ps 73:26). Happy you, said the apostle to his disciples, who have been robbed of your goods for the sake of Jesus Christ. "You even joined in the sufferings of those who were in prison and joyfully assented to the confiscation of your goods, knowing that you had better and more permanent possessions" (Heb 10:34). The saint is not afflicted at bidding an eternal farewell to honors, for he always hated them, and considered them to be what they really are — smoke and vanity. He is not afflicted in leaving relatives, for he loved them only in God, and at death he recommends them to his heavenly Father, who loves them more than he does; and having a secure confidence of salvation, he expects to be better able to assist them from heaven than on this earth. In a word, he who has constantly said during life, My God and my all, continues to repeat it with greater consolation and greater tenderness at the hour of death.

(Preparation VIII)

"The time is short: those who make use of the world as though they were not using it, for the world as we know it is passing away" (1 Cor 7:31). What is our life on this earth but a scene, which passes away and ends very soon? "The world as we know it is passing away." "The world," says Cornelius á Lapide, "is like a stage; one generation passes away, another comes." Who acts the part of a king, takes not the purple with him. Tell me, O villa, O house, how many masters have you had? When the comedy is over, the king is no longer king; the master ceases to be master. You at present are in possession of such a villa and palace; but death will come, and they will pass to other masters.

"A moment's affliction brings forgetfulness of past delights" (Sir 11:27). The gloomy hour of death brings to an end and makes us forget all the grandeur, nobility, and pomp of the world. Casimir, king of Poland, while he sat at a table with the nobles of his kingdom, died in the act of raising a cup to take a draught; and the scene ended for him. In seven days after his election, the Emperor Celsus was killed, and the scene closed for Celsus. Ladislaus, king of Poland, in his eighteenth year, while he was preparing for the reception of his bride, the daughter of the king of France, was suddenly seized with a violent pain, which soon deprived him of life. Couriers were instantly despatched to announce to her that the scene was over for Ladislaus, and that she might return to France. By meditating on the vanity of the world, Francis Borgia became a saint. At the sight of the Empress Isabella, who had died in the midst of worldly grandeur and in the flower of youth, he, as has been already said, resolved to give himself entirely to God. "Thus, then," he said, "end the grandeurs and crowns of this world: I will henceforth serve a master who can never die."

Let us endeavor to live in such a manner that what was said to the fool in the gospel may not be said to us at the hour of death: "You fool! This very night your life shall be required of you. To whom will all this piled-up wealth of yours go?" (Lk 12:20). Hence, the Redeemer adds: "That is the way it works with the man who grows rich for himself instead of growing rich in the sight of God" (Lk 12:21). Again he tells you to acquire the riches, not of the world, but of God—of virtues and merits, which are goods which shall remain with you for eternity in heaven. "Make it your practice instead to store up heavenly treasure, which neither moths nor rust corrode nor thieves break in and steal" (Mt 6:20). Let us then labor to acquire the great treasure of divine love. "What," says St. Augustine, "has the rich man, if he has not charity? What does the poor man want, if he has charity?" If a person had all the riches in the world, and has not God, he or she is the poorest of all. But the poor person who possesses God, possesses all things. And who are they that possess God? "He," says St. John, "who abides in love abides in God, and God in him" (1 Jn 4:16).

(*Preparation* XIII)

St. Thomas teaches that every act of love merits for the soul eternal life. Why then should we envy the great ones of the earth? If we are in the grace of God, we can constantly acquire far more greatness in heaven. Moreover, who has experienced it, can conceive the peace which only a soul in the grace of God enjoys in this life. "Taste and see how good the Lord is" (Ps 34:9).

(*Preparation* XIX)

God has certainly not placed us in this world to become rich, or acquire honors, or to indulge our senses but to gain eternal life. "Your benefit is sanctification as you tend toward eternal life" (Rom 6:22). And nothing but the attainment of this end is of importance to us. "One thing only is required" (Lk 10:41). But there is nothing that sinners despise more than this end: they think only of the present; they each day walk toward death, and approach the gate of eternity, but know not where they are going. "What would you think," says St. Augustine, "of a pilot, who, when asked where he is going should answer, that he did not know? Would not all exclaim, that he is bringing the ship to ruin?"

(*Preparation* XX)

In this life all people seek after peace. The merchant, the soldier, the person who goes to law, labor with the hope of making a fortune, and of thus finding peace, by worldly fortune, by a more exalted post, by gaining a lawsuit. But poor worldlings seek from the world that peace which the world cannot give. God alone can give us peace. The holy Church prays in the following words: "Give to your servants that peace which the world cannot give." No; the world with all its goods cannot content the human heart for we were created not for them, but for God alone: hence God alone can make us happy and content. Brute animals, that have been made for sensual delights, find peace in earthly goods. Give to an ox a bundle of hay, and to a dog a piece of flesh, and they are content, they desire nothing more. But the soul that has been created for no other end than to love God, and to live in union with him, will never be able to find peace or happiness in sensual enjoyments: God alone can make it perfectly content.

(*Preparation* XXI)

MARY

O how sweet it will be when it comes time to die—to know that we
have contributed to bringing devotion to Mary into people's hearts.

These words of St. Alphonsus take us right to the heart of his life-long
zeal to make the Madonna better known and loved. *The Glories of Mary,*
which he published in 1750, one of his first major works, was the fruit of
sixteen years of hard work since his goal was to collect the best Marian
quotes from scripture, theology, and tradition, and present it in a popular
way. Did he succeed? This one work has gone into well over one thousand
editions in the majority of the languages of the world.

He tells his readers that he wanted to stress two of Mary's qualities in
particular, leaving her other prerogatives to other writers. Thus, his focus
is primarily on Mary's *mercy* and her powerful *intercession.* The format
which he chose is very similar to that of *The Practice of the Love of Jesus
Christ;* namely, it is a commentary on the *Salve Regina,* the Hail Holy
Queen. The second half of the work is dedicated to an explanation of her
feasts and some of her better-known titles. And, again, we find the tender
Alphonsian prayers at the end of each chapter. In writing these prayers he
is obviously wearing his heart on his sleeve.

However, his Marian devotion and the unctuous prayers are not just
the overflow of his own personal relationship with Mary; she was always
his "Mamma Maria!" They flow from a deeply theological and ecclesias-
tical vision of Mary's God-given role in his plan of redemption and her
role within the Church. From his familiarity with the history and tradition
of the Church he was convinced that both the Church and the individual
are always much poorer during those times when the Mary-factor in
Christian faith is neglected or down-played. And he was a man of his own
age, an age which felt the backwash of both Protestantism's and
Jansenism's devaluation of devotion to Mary. The latter particularly irked
him with its disembodied spirituality and the consequent taboo on the
emotions, affections, and the maternal and feminine elements in the
theology of redemption and of the Church. He did not express surprise at
the controversy which surrounded this book shortly after it was published,
a position that continued down into the nineteenth century. The criticism

centered not just on the fact that he did use some stories and legends that were a bit fantastic and surely unhistorical but, more importantly, some felt that he was, in his glorification of Mary, taking away from Christ's role as unique and universal Savior. One of the titles which he championed is "Mary, Mediatrix of all Graces," and it was this title which caused the difficulty. However, it is obvious from a reading of the text, that he was careful to make a clear distinction between Jesus' universal *mediation of justice through merit* and Mary's *mediation of grace through intercession.* There is only one Redeemer, one Savior, and his name is Christ. Properly understood, *The Glories of Mary* are not an expression of Mariolatry. Liguori's doctrine is, as usual, solid and four-square in line with the teaching of the Church. Indeed, he himself was concerned with "indiscreet" devotions to Mary, devotions that did not lead people to Mary's Son. It is interesting that in his whole lifetime of almost ninety-one years, he made just one pilgrimage to a Marian shrine, numerous as they were in Italy, and that was as a side trip to his episcopal consecration in Rome; namely, a visit to the shrine of Our Lady of Loretto. With this in mind, we now end by quoting from Liguori's own "Note to the Reader":

In the introduction referring to the fifth chapter of this work (a chapter called "Mary Mediatress"), I say that it is the will of God that all graces should come to us by the hands of Mary. Now, this is, indeed, a consoling truth for souls tenderly devoted to our most blessed lady, and for poor sinners who wish to repent.

Nor should this opinion be looked upon as contrary to sound doctrine, since the Father of theology, St. Augustine, in common with most writers, says that Mary cooperated, by her charity, in the spiritual birth of all members of the Church. A celebrated writer, one who cannot be accused of exaggeration or misguided devotion, says, "that it was, properly speaking, on Calvary that Jesus founded his Church"; and it is evident that Mary cooperated in a most special manner in the accomplishment of this work.

And now, to say all in a few words: God, in order to glorify the mother of the Redeemer, has so determined and disposed that of her general charity she should intercede on behalf of all those for whom his Son paid the price of our redemption and for whom he offered that superabundant price of his precious blood which alone is our salvation.

On this doctrine, and on all that is in accord with it, I ground my own propositions, propositions which the saints have not hesitated to assert in their tender colloquies with Mary and in their discourses in her honor.

One final observation! On the personal level, Liguori's favorite Madonna was Our Lady of Good Counsel. I have often wondered if this was because of his youthful years of scrupulosity and indecision. At any rate, this was the Madonna who accompanied him from Naples to the poverty-stricken hills of Scala and then into the mountains of St. Agatha of the Goths where he was bishop and, finally, back to Nocera di Pagani, where he died with her picture beside him and just as the Angelus was ringing.

However, when Alphonsus began his own religious institute, the Congregation of the Most Holy Redeemer, he chose as its patroness Mary, the Immaculate Conception. He immediately saw the connection between this prerogative of Mary and the motto that he had chosen for the Redemptorists: "With him is plentiful redemption." And among all the members of the human race, Mary was the paragon of plentiful redemption, immaculate from the very moment of her conception; redeemed by the grace of Christ but in a preventive way, which is to say that the original sin which is removed from us was never allowed to touch her.

In the second part of *The Glories of Mary,* writing of the feast of the Immaculate Conception, he makes the three following points:

1. It was befitting that each of the three Divine Persons should preserve Mary from original sin . . .

2. It was becoming that the Son should preserve Mary from sin, as being his mother . . .

3. It was becoming that the Holy Spirit should preserve her as his spouse.

This is followed by ten pages of "theological proofs" of the Immaculate Conception. Indeed, so dedicated to this extraordinary gift given by God to Mary was Liguori that, from the earliest days of his congregation, the members were required by vow to defend the Immaculate Conception. Mind you, the doctrine had not yet been defined by the Church as a *De Fide* teaching—that was only to come over a hundred years later. However, when it was finally defined, Alphonsus Liguori's teachings on this Marian prerogative, as presented in *The Glories of Mary,* were highly instrumental in moving Pius IX and the First Vatican Council to their final affirmative vote.

The Glories of Mary

My beloved reader and brother or sister in Mary: Since the devotion that led me to write, and moves you to read, this book makes us happy children of the same good mother, should you hear it remarked that I might have spared myself the labor, as there are already so many celebrated and learned works on the same subject, I beg that you will reply, in the words of the Abbot Francone, that "the praise of Mary is an inexhaustible fount: the more it is enlarged the fuller it gets, and the more you fill it so much the more is it enlarged." In short, this Blessed Virgin is so great and so sublime that the more she is praised the more there remains to praise; so much so, says an ancient writer, "that if all the tongues of people were put together, and even if each of their members was changed into a tongue, they would not suffice to praise her as much as she deserves."

(Glories, Introduction)

It is not without a meaning, or by chance, that Mary's clients call her mother; and indeed they seem unable to invoke her under any other name, and never tire of calling her mother. Mother, yes! for she is truly our mother; not indeed carnally, but spiritually; of our souls and of our salvation.

Sin, by depriving our souls of divine grace, deprived them also of life. Jesus our Redeemer, with an excess of mercy and love, came to restore this life by his own death on the cross, as he himself declared: "I came that they might have life and have it to the full" (Jn 10:10). He says "to the full"; for, according to theologians, the benefit of redemption far exceeded the injury done by Adam's sin. So that by reconciling us with God he made himself the Father of souls in the law of grace, as it was foretold by the prophet Isaiah; "They name him Wonder-Counselor, God-Hero, Father-Forever, Prince of Peace" (Is 9:5). But if Jesus is the Father of our souls, Mary is also their mother; for she, by giving us Jesus, gave us true life; and afterwards, by offering the life of her Son on Mount Calvary for our salvation, she brought us forth to the life of grace.

It is true that, according to the prophecy of Isaiah, Jesus, in dying for the redemption of the human race, chose to be alone. "The wine press I have trodden alone" (Is 63:3); but, seeing the ardent desire of Mary to aid in the salvation of humankind, he disposed it so that she, by the sacrifice and offering of the life of her Jesus, should co-operate in our salvation, and thus become the mother of our souls. This our Savior signified, when, before expiring, he looked down from the cross on his mother and on the disciple St. John, who stood at its foot, and, first addressing Mary, he said, "There is your son" (Jn 19:26); saying, Behold, the whole human race, which by the offer you make of my life for the salvation of all, is even now being born to the life of grace. Then turning to the disciple, he said, "There is your mother" (Jn 19:27). "By these words," says St. Bernardine of Sienna, "Mary, by reason of the love she bore them, became the mother, not only of St. John, but of all people." And Silveira remarks, that St. John himself, in stating this fact in his gospel, says: "Then he said to the disciple, 'There is your mother.' " Here observe well that Jesus Christ did not address himself to John, but to the disciple, in order to show that he then gave Mary to all who are his disciples. And what mother, exclaims St. Bonaventure, loves her children, and attends to their welfare, as you love us and care for us, O most sweet Queen! "For do you not love us and seek our welfare far more without comparison than any earthly mother?"

"If those who pray," says St. Anselm, "do not merit to be heard, the merits of the mother, to whom they recommend themselves will intercede effectually."

Therefore, St. Bernard exhorts all sinners to have recourse to Mary, invoking her with great confidence; for though the sinner does not merit the graces which he or she asks, yet he or she receives them, because this Blessed Virgin asks and obtains them from God. . . . "This would be the duty of a good mother. And thus it is," the saint goes on to say, "that Mary acts; for she is the mother of Jesus, and the mother of humanity. When she sees a sinner at enmity with Jesus Christ, she cannot endure it, and does all in her power to make peace between them.

(*Glories* I, I)

Let us then conclude in the words of St. Bernard: "O human beings, whoever you are, understand that in this world you are tossed about on a stormy and tempestuous sea, rather than walking on solid ground; remember that if you would avoid being drowned, you must never turn your eyes from the brightness of this star, but keep them fixed on it, and call on

Mary. In dangers, in straits, in doubts, remember Mary, invoke Mary." Yes, in dangers of sinning, when molested by temptations, when doubtful as to how you should act, remember that Mary can help you; and call upon her, and she will instantly succor you. "Let not her name leave your lips, let it be ever in your heart." Your hearts should never lose confidence in her holy name, nor should your lips ever cease to invoke it. "Following her, you will certainly not go astray." O, no, if we follow Mary, we shall never err from the paths of salvation. "Imploring her you will not despair." Each time that we invoke her aid, we shall be inspired with perfect confidence. "If she supports you, you cannot fall"; "if she protects you, you have nothing to fear, for you cannot be lost": "with her for your guide, you will not be weary; for your salvation will be worked out with ease." "If she is propitious, you will gain the port." If Mary undertakes our defence, we are certain of gaining the kingdom of heaven. "Do this and you shall live" (Lk 10:28).

The prophet Isaiah tells us that when a person is on the point of leaving the world, hell is opened and sends forth its most terrible demons, both to tempt the soul before it leaves the body, and also to accuse it when presented before the tribunal of Jesus Christ for judgment. The prophet says, "The nether world below is all astir preparing for your coming, it awakens the shades to greet you" (Is 14:9). But Richard of St. Laurence remarks that when the soul is defended by Mary, the devils dare not even accuse it, knowing that the judge never condemned, and never will condemn, a soul protected by his august mother. He asks, "Who would dare accuse one who is patronized by the mother of him who is to judge?" Mary not only assists her beloved servants at death and encourages them, but she herself accompanies them to the tribunal-seat of God.

As St. Jerome says, writing to the virgin Eustochia, "What a day of joy will that be for you, when Mary the mother of our Lord, accompanied by choirs of virgins, will go to meet you." The Blessed Virgin assured St. Bridget of this; for, speaking of her devout clients at the point of death, she said, "Then will I, their dear lady and mother, fly to them, that they may have consolation and refreshment." St. Vincent Ferrer says, that not only does the most Blessed Virgin console and refresh them, but that "she receives the souls of the dying."

(*Glories* I, II)

She is the mother who gives birth to holy hope in our hearts; not to the hope of the vain and transitory goods of this life, but of the immense and eternal goods of heaven.

"Hail, then, O hope of my soul!" exclaims St. Ephrem, addressing this divine mother; "hail, O certain salvation of Christians; hail, O helper of the world!" Other saints remind us, that after God, our only hope is Mary; and therefore they call her, "after God, their only hope."

St. Ephrem, reflecting on the present order of providence, by which God wills (as St. Bernard says, and as we shall prove at length) that all who are saved should be saved by the means of Mary, thus addresses her: "O Lady, cease not to watch over us; preserve and guard us under the wings of your compassion and mercy, for, after God, we have no hope but in you." St. Thomas of Villanova repeats the same thing, calling her "our only refuge, help, and asylum." St. Bernard seems to give the reason for this when he says, "See, O humans, the designs of God—designs by which he is able to dispense his mercy more abundantly to us, for, desiring to redeem the whole human race, he has placed the whole price of redemption in the hands of Mary, that she may dispense it at will."

One of the titles which is the most encouraging to poor sinners, and under which the Church teaches us to invoke Mary in the Litany of Loretto, is that of "Refuge of Sinners." In Judea in ancient times there were cities of refuge, in which criminals who fled there for protection were exempt from the punishments which they had deserved. Nowadays these cities are not so numerous; there is but one, and that is Mary, of whom the psalmist says "Glorious things are said of you, O city of God" (Ps 87:3). But this city differs from the ancient ones in this respect—that in the latter all kinds of criminals did not find refuge, nor was the protection extended to every class of crime; but under the mantle of Mary all sinners, without exception, find refuge for every sin that they may have committed, provided only that they go there to seek for this protection. "I am the city of refuge," says St. John Damascene, in the name of our Queen, "to all who fly to me." And it is sufficient to have recourse to her, for whoever has the good fortune to enter this city need not speak to be saved. "Let us form ranks and enter the walled cities" (Jer 8:14). . . . For if we do not presume to ask our Lord to forgive us, it will suffice to enter this city and be silent, for Mary will speak and ask all that we require.

It is related in the sacred scriptures that Booz allowed Ruth "to gather the gleanings into sheaves after the harvesters" (Ru 2:7). Bonaventure says, "that as Ruth found favor with Booz, so has Mary found favor with our Lord, and is also allowed to gather the ears of corn after the reapers. The reapers followed by Mary are all evangelical laborers, missionaries, preachers, and confessors, who are constantly reaping souls for God. But there are some hardened and rebellious souls which are abandoned even by these. To Mary alone it is granted to save them by her powerful intercession." Truly unfortunate are they if they do not allow themselves to be gathered, even by this sweet lady. They will indeed be most certainly lost and accursed. But, on the other hand, blessed are they who have recourse to this good mother. "There is not in the world," says the devout Blosius, "any sinner, however revolting and wicked, who is despised or rejected by Mary; she can, she wills, and she knows how to reconcile him or her to her most beloved Son, if only he or she will seek her assistance."

(Glories I, III)

No one denies that Jesus Christ is our only mediator of justice, and that he by his merits has obtained our reconciliation with God. But, on the other hand, it is impious to assert that God is not pleased to grant graces at the intercession of his saints, and more especially of Mary his mother, whom Jesus desires so much to see loved and honored by all. Who can pretend that the honor bestowed on a mother does not redound to the honor of the son? "The glory of children is their parentage" (Prv 17:6). Whence St. Bernard says, "Let us not imagine that we obscure the glory of the Son by the great praise we lavish on the mother; for the more she is honored, the greater is the glory of her Son." . . . There can be no doubt that by the merits of Jesus, Mary was made the mediatress of our salvation; not indeed a mediatress of justice, but of grace and intercession; as St. Bonaventure expressly calls her "Mary, the most faithful mediatress of our salvation." And St. Laurence Justinian asks, "How can she be otherwise than full of grace, who has been made the ladder to paradise, the gate of heaven, the most true mediatress between God and the human being?"

Hence the learned Suarez justly remarks, that if we implore our blessed lady to obtain us a favor, it is not because we distrust the divine mercy, but rather that we fear our own unworthiness and the absence of proper dispositions; and we recommend ourselves to Mary, that her dignity may supply for our lowliness. He says that we apply to Mary "in order that the dignity of the intercessor may supply for our misery."

We willingly admit that God is the source of every good, and the absolute master of all graces; and that Mary is only a pure creature, who receives whatever she obtains as a pure favor from God. But who can ever deny that it is most reasonable and proper to assert that God, in order to exalt this great creature, who more than all others honored and loved him during her life, and whom, moreover, he had chosen to be the mother of his Son, our common Redeemer, wills that all graces that are granted to those whom he has redeemed should pass through and be dispensed by the hands of Mary? We most readily admit that Jesus Christ is the only mediator of justice, according to the distinction just made, and that by his merits he obtains us all graces and salvation; but we say that Mary is the mediatress of grace; and that receiving all she obtains through Jesus Christ, and because she prays and asks for it in the name of Jesus Christ, yet all the same whatever graces we receive, they come to us through her intercession.

St. Bernard says "that God has filled Mary with all graces, so that people may receive by her means, as by a channel, every good thing that comes to them." . . . On this the saint makes the following significant remark: "Before the birth of the Blessed Virgin, a constant flow of graces was wanting, because this aqueduct did not exist." But now that Mary has been given to the world, heavenly graces constantly flow through her on all.

Again, the holy Church calls her "the happy gate of heaven;" for as the same St. Bernard remarks: "As every mandate of grace that is sent by a king passes through the palace-gates, so does every grace that comes from heaven to the world pass through the hands of Mary." St. Bonaventure says that Mary is called "the gate of heaven, because no one can enter that blessed kingdom without passing through her." "As God was pleased to dwell in the womb of this holy Virgin, she acquired, so to speak, a kind of jurisdiction over all graces; for when Jesus Christ issued forth from her most sacred womb, all the streams of divine gifts flowed from her as from a celestial ocean." Elsewhere, repeating the same idea in more distinct terms, he asserts that "from the moment that this Virgin Mother conceived the divine Word in her womb, she acquired a special jurisdiction, so to say, over all the gifts of the Holy Spirit, so that no creature has since received any grace from God otherwise than through the hands of Mary."

St. Bernard says, "that as a man and a woman cooperated in our ruin, so it was proper that another man and another woman should cooperate in our redemption, and these two were Jesus and his mother Mary." "There is no doubt," says the saint, "that Jesus Christ alone was more than sufficient to redeem us; but it was more becoming that both sexes should cooperate in the reparation of an evil in causing which both had shared." Hence Blessed Albert the Great calls Mary, the "helper of redemption. . . ." This is confirmed by St. Anselm, who says, "that although God could create the world out of nothing, yet, when it was lost by sin, he would not repair the evil without the cooperation of Mary."

"But," says the modern author already quoted [Louis A. Muratori], "if all graces come through Mary, when we implore the intercession of other saints, they must have recourse to the mediation of Mary. But that," he says, "no one believes or ever dreamed."

As to believing it, I reply that in that there can be no error or difficulty. What difficulty can there be in saying that God, in order to honor his mother, and having made her Queen of saints, and willing that all graces shall be dispensed by her hands, should also will that the saints should address themselves to her to obtain favors for their clients?

And as to saying that no one ever dreamed of such a thing, I find that St. Bernard, St. Anselm, St. Bonaventure, Suarez, and others, expressly declare it to be the case. "In vain," says St. Bernard, "would a person ask other saints for a favor, if Mary did not interpose to obtain it." Some other author, explaining the words of the psalm, "the rich among the people seek your favor" (45:13), says, that "the saints are the rich of that great people of God, who, when they wish to obtain a favor from God for their clients, recommend themselves to Mary, and she immediately obtains it." And Father Suarez correctly remarks, "that we beg the saints to be our intercessors with Mary, because she is their Queen and sovereign lady." Whoever places his or her confidence in a creature independently of God, he or she certainly is cursed by God; for God is the only source and dispenser of every good, and the creature without God is nothing, and can give nothing. But if our Lord has so disposed it, as we have already proved that he has done, that all graces should pass through Mary as by a channel of mercy, we not only can but ought to assert that she, by whose means we receive the divine graces, is truly our hope.

Let us, then, in the words of St. Bernard, "endeavor to venerate this divine mother with the whole affection of our hearts; for such is the will of God, who is pleased that we should receive every good thing from her hand." And therefore the saint exhorts us, whenever we desire or ask for any grace, to recommend ourselves to Mary, and to be assured that we shall receive it by her means.

                                                              (*Glories* I, V)

"If then, O brethren," concludes Thomas à Kempis, "you desire consolation in every labor, have recourse to Mary; invoke the name of Mary, honor Mary, recommend yourselves to Mary, rejoice with Mary, weep with Mary, pray with Mary, walk with Mary, seek Jesus with Mary; in fine, desire to live and die with Jesus and Mary. By acting thus you will always advance in the ways of God, for Mary will most willingly pray for you, and the Son will most certainly grant all that his mother asks."

Let us then, O devout reader, beg God to grant us, that at death the name of Mary may be the last word on our lips. This was the prayer of St. Germanus: "May the last movement of my tongue be to pronounce the name of the Mother of God."

                                                              (*Glories* I, X)

"Humility," says St. Bernard, "is the foundation and guardian of virtues"; and with reason, for without it no other virtue can exist in a soul. Should she possess all virtues, all will depart when humility is gone. But, on the other hand, as St. Francis de Sales wrote to St. Jane Frances de Chantal, "God so loves humility, that whenever he sees it, he is immediately drawn thither." This beautiful and so necessary virtue was unknown in the world; but the Son of God himself came on earth to teach it by his own example, and willed that in that virtue in particular we should endeavor to imitate him: "Learn from me, for I am gentle and humble of heart" (Mt 11:29). Mary, being the first and most perfect disciple of Jesus Christ in the practice of all virtues, was the first also in that of humility, and by it merited to be exalted above all creatures.

Not indeed that Mary considered herself a sinner: for humility is truth, as St. Teresa remarks: and Mary knew that she had never offended God, nor was it that she did not acknowledge that she had received greater graces from God than all other creatures; for a humble heart always acknowledges the special favors of the Lord, to humble herself the more: but the divine mother, by the greater light wherewith she knew the infinite greatness and goodness of God, also knew her own nothingness, and therefore, more than all others, humbled herself, saying with the sacred Spouse: "Do not stare at me because I am swarthy, because the sun has burned me" (Sg 1:6).

Moreover, it is an act of humility to conceal heavenly gifts. Mary wished to conceal from St. Joseph the great favor whereby she had become the Mother of God, although it seemed necessary to make it known to him, if only to remove from the mind of her poor spouse any suspicions as to her virtue, which he might have entertained on seeing her pregnant: or at least the perplexity in which it indeed threw him. For St. Joseph, on the one hand unwilling to doubt Mary's chastity, and on the other ignorant of the mystery, "decided to divorce her quietly" (Mt 1:19). This he would have done, had not the angel revealed to him that his spouse was pregnant by the operation of the Holy Spirit.

Again, a soul that is truly humble refuses her own praise; and should praises be bestowed on her, she refers them all to God. Behold, Mary is disturbed at hearing herself praised by St. Gabriel; and when St. Elizabeth said, "Blest are you among women. . . But who am I that the mother of my Lord should come to me?. . . Blest is she who trusted" (Lk 1:42, 43, 45), Mary referred all to God, and answered in that humble canticle, "My being proclaims the greatness of the Lord" (Lk 1:46). "You praise me, Elizabeth; but I praise the Lord, to whom alone honor is due. You wonder that I should come to you, and I wonder at the divine goodness in which alone my spirit exults": "My spirit finds joy in God my Savior" (Lk 1:47). You praise me because I have believed; I praise my God, because he has been pleased to exalt my nothingness: "For he has looked upon his servant in her lowliness" (Lk 1:48).

There can be no doubt, as St. Gregory of Nyssa remarks, that of all virtues there is perhaps none the practice of which is more difficult to our nature, corrupted as it is by sin, than that of humility. But there is no escape; we can never be true children of Mary if we are not humble. "If," says St. Bernard, "you cannot imitate the virginity of this humble Virgin, imitate her humility." She detests the proud, and invites only the humble to come to her: "Let whoever is simple turn in here" (Prv 9:4).

(Glories IV, I)

So great was Mary's charity when on earth, that she succored the needy without even being asked; as was the case at the marriage-feast of Cana, when she told her Son that family's distress, "They have no more wine" (Jn 2:3), and asked him to work a miracle. Oh, with what speed did she fly when there was question of relieving her neighbor! When she went to the house of Elizabeth to fulfil an office of charity, "Mary set out, proceeding in haste into the hill country" (Lk 1:39). She could not, however, more fully display the greatness of her charity than she did in the offering which she made of her Son to death for our salvation. On this subject St. Bonaventure says, "Mary so loved the world as to give her only-begotten Son." Hence St. Anselm exclaims, "O blessed amongst women, your purity surpasses that of the angels, and your compassion that of the saints!" "Nor has this love of Mary for us," says St. Bonaventure, "diminished now that she is in heaven, but it has increased; for now she better sees the miseries of humanity." And therefore the saint goes on to say: "Great was the mercy of Mary toward the wretched when she was still in exile on earth; but far greater is it now that she reigns in heaven."

(*Glories* IV, III)

As the Blessed Virgin is the mother of holy love and hope, so also is she the mother of faith. . . . And with reason is she so, says St. Irenaeus; for "the evil done by Eve's incredulity was remedied by Mary's faith." This is confirmed by Tertullian, who says that because Eve, contrary to the assurance she had received from God, believed the serpent, she brought death into the world; but our Queen, because she believed the angel when he said that she, remaining a virgin, would become the mother of God, brought salvation into the world. For St. Augustine says, that "when Mary consented to the incarnation of the eternal Word, by means of her faith she opened heaven to humanity." Richard, on the words of St. Paul, "The unbelieving husband is consecrated by his believing wife" (1 Cor 7:14), also says, that "Mary is the believing woman by whose faith the unbelieving Adam and all his posterity are saved." Hence, on account of her faith Elizabeth called the holy Virgin blessed: "Blest is she who trusted that the Lord's words to her would be fulfilled" (Lk 1:45). And St. Augustine adds, that Mary was rather blessed by receiving the faith of Christ than by conceiving the flesh of Christ.

Father Suarez says, that the most holy Virgin had more faith than all people and angels. She saw her Son in the crib of Bethlehem, and believed him the Creator of the world. She saw him fly from Herod, and yet believed him the King of kings. She saw him born and believed him eternal. She saw him poor and in need of food, and believed him the Lord of the universe. She saw him lying on straw, and believed him omnipotent. She observed that he did not speak, and she believed him infinite wisdom. She heard him weep, and believed him the joy of paradise. In fine, she saw him in death, despised and crucified, and, although faith wavered in others, Mary remained firm in the belief that he was God.

On these words of the gospel, "Near the cross of Jesus there stood his mother" (Jn 19:25), St. Antoninus says, "Mary stood, supported by her faith, which she retained firm in the divinity of Christ." And for this reason it is, the saint adds, that in the office of *Tenebrae* only one candle is left lighted. St. Leo, on this subject, applies to our blessed lady the words of Proverbs, "At night her lamp is undimmed" (31:19).

Therefore Mary merited by her great faith to become "the light of all the faithful," as St. Methodius calls her; and the "Queen of the true faith," as she is called by St. Cyril of Alexandria. The holy Church herself attributes to the merits of Mary's faith the destruction of all heresies: "Rejoice, O Virgin Mary, for you alone have destroyed all heresies throughout the world." St. Thomas of Villanova, explaining the words of the Holy Spirit "You have ravished my heart, my sister, my bride with one glance of your eyes" (Sg 4:9), says that "these eyes denoted Mary's faith, by which she greatly pleased the Son of God."

But how can we imitate Mary's faith? Faith, at the same time that it is a gift, is also a virtue. It is a gift of God, inasmuch as it is a light infused by him into our souls; and a virtue, inasmuch as the soul has to exercise itself in the practice of it. Hence faith is not only to be the rule of our belief, but also that of our actions; therefore St. Gregory says, "Those truly believe who put what they believe into practice;" and St. Augustine, "You say I believe; do what you say, and it is faith." This is to have a lively faith to live according to our belief: "My just man will live by faith" (Heb 10:38). Thus did the Blessed Virgin live very differently from those who do not live in accordance with what they believe, and whose faith is dead as St. James declares, "Faith without works is as dead as a body without breath" (Jas 2:26).

Diogenes sought for a wise man on earth; but God, amongst the many faithful, seems to seek for a Christian, for few there are who have good works; the greater part have only the name of Christian. To such as these should be applied the words once addressed by Alexander to a cowardly soldier who was also named Alexander: "Either change your name or change your conduct." But as Father Avila used to say, "It would be better to shut up these poor creatures as madmen, believing, as they do, that an eternity of happiness is prepared for those who lead good lives, and an eternity of misery for those who lead bad ones, and who yet live as if they believed nothing." St. Augustine therefore exhorts us to see things with the eyes of Christians, that is to say, with eyes which look at all in the light of faith; for, as St. Teresa often said, all sins come from a want of faith. Let us therefore entreat the most holy Virgin, by the merit of her faith, to obtain us a lively faith. "O Lady, increase our faith."

(Glories IV, IV)

Since the fall of Adam, the senses being rebellious to reason, chastity is of all virtues the one that is the most difficult to practice. St. Augustine says: "Of all the combats in which we are engaged, the most severe are those of chastity; its battles are of daily occurrence, but victory is rare." May God be ever praised, however, who in Mary has given us a great example of this virtue.

"With reason," says Blessed Albertus Magnus, "is Mary called the Virgin of virgins; for she, without the counsel or example of others, was the first who offered her virginity to God." Thus did she bring all virgins who imitate her to God, as David had already foretold: "Behind her the virgins of her train are brought to you. . . they enter the palace of the king" (Ps 45:15-16). Without counsel and without example. Yes; for St. Bernard says: "O Virgin, who taught you to please God by virginity, and to lead an angel's life on earth?" "Ah," replies St. Sophronius, "God chose this most pure virgin for his mother, that she might be an example of chastity to all."

St. John Damascene says, that Mary "is pure and a lover of purity." Hence she cannot endure those who are unchaste. But whoever has recourse to her will certainly be delivered from this vice, if he or she only pronounces her name with confidence.

(Glories IV, VII)

When the angel Gabriel announced to Mary God's great designs upon her, she, through love for obedience would only call herself a handmaid: "I am the servant of the Lord" (Lk 1:38). "Yes," says St. Thomas of Villanova, "for this faithful handmaid never, in either thought or word or deed, contradicted the Most High; but, entirely despoiled of her own will, she lived always and in all things obedient to that of God." She herself declared that God was pleased with her obedience, when she said, "He has regarded the humility of his handmaid"; for in prompt obedience it is that the humility of a servant, properly speaking consists.

But above all she showed her heroic obedience when, to obey the divine will, she offered her Son to death; and this with such constancy, as St. Anselm and St. Antoninus say, that had executioners been wanting, she would have been ready herself to have crucified him. Hence Venerable Bede, explaining our Lord's answer to the woman spoken of in the gospel, who exclaimed, "Blest is the womb that bore you" . . . "Rather" he replied, "blest are they who hear the word of God and keep it" (Lk 11:27), says that Mary was indeed blessed in becoming the mother of God, but that she was much more so in always loving and obeying the divine will.

For this reason, all who love obedience are highly pleasing to the Blessed Virgin.

(*Glories* IV, VIII)

This world being a place of merit, is rightly called a valley of tears; for we are all placed in it to suffer, that we may, by patience, gain our own souls unto life eternal, as our Lord himself says, "By patient endurance you will save your lives" (Lk 21:19). God gave us the Blessed Virgin Mary as a model of all virtues, but more especially as an example of patience. St. Francis de Sales, amongst other things, remarks, that it was precisely for this reason that at the marriage-feast of Cana Jesus Christ gave the Blessed Virgin an answer, by which he seemed to value her prayers but little: "Woman, how does this concern of yours involve me?" (Jn 2:4). And he did this that he might give us the example of the patience of his most holy mother. But what need have we to seek for instances of this virtue? Mary's whole life was a continual exercise of her patience. . . . Compassion alone for the Redeemer's sufferings sufficed to make her a martyr of patience. Hence St. Bonaventure says, "that a crucified mother conceived a crucified Son." In speaking of her dolors, we have already considered how much she suffered, both in her journey to Egypt, and during her residence there, as also during the time she lived with her Son in the house at Nazareth. What Mary endured when present at the death of Jesus on Calvary is alone sufficient to show us how constant and sublime was her patience: "There stood by the cross of Jesus his mother."

Then it was that precisely by the merit of her patience, as Blessed Albert the Great says, she brought us forth to the life of grace.

If we, then, wish to be the children of Mary, we must endeavor to imitate her in her patience: "For what," says St. Cyprian, "can enrich us with greater merit in this life, and greater glory in the next, than the patient enduring of sufferings?" God said, by the prophet Hosea, "I will have no pity on her children" (2:6). To this St. Gregory adds, that "the way of the elect is hedged with thorns." As a hedge of thorns protects a vineyard, so does God protect his servants from the danger of attaching themselves to the earth, by encompassing them with tribulations. Therefore St. Cyprian concludes that it is patience that delivers us from sin and from hell.

It is also patience that makes saints: "Let endurance come to its perfection" (Jas 1:4), bearing in peace, not only the crosses which come immediately from God, such as sickness, poverty, but also those which come from people—persecutions, injuries, and the rest. St. John saw all the saints bearing palm branches—the emblem of martyrdom—in their hands; "After this I saw before me a huge crowd holding palm branches in their hands" (Rev 7:9); thereby denoting that all adults who are saved must be martyrs, either by shedding their blood for Christ or by patience. "Rejoice then," exclaims St. Gregory; "we can be martyrs without the executioner's sword, if we only preserve patience." "Provided only," as St. Bernard says, "we endure the afflictions of this life with patience and joy." O what fruit will not every pain borne for God's sake produce for us in heaven! Hence the apostle encourages us, saying, "The present burden of our trial is light enough and earns for us an eternal weight of glory beyond all comparison" (2 Cor 4:17).

St. Teresa's instructions on this subject are beautiful. She used to say, "Those who embrace the cross do not feel it;" and elsewhere, "that if we resolve to suffer the pain ceases." When our crosses weigh heavily upon us, let us have recourse to Mary, who is called by the Church "the Comfortress of the afflicted"; and by St. John Damascene, "the Remedy for all sorrows of the heart."

(*Glories* IV, IX)

CHRONOLOGICAL TABLE

1696   September 27. Alphonsus is born to Giuseppe de' Liguori and Anna de' Cavalieri in a small suburb of Naples, Italy, called Marianella.

In the years to follow he receives classical education at home and is involved in the activities of the Youth Confraternity of the Oratory which had grown up around St. Philip Neri (1515-1595) a century and a half earlier.

1708   Begins his studies of canon and civil law at the university of Naples.

1712   Alphonsus graduates from law school and begins practice. Every week he helps the sick in the hospital and he keeps up his frequent visits to the Blessed Sacrament and his devotion to Mary. He afterward attributes these practices to his conversion.

1715   Becomes a noted lawyer; in his legal career he loses only one case and subsequently abandons the legal profession.

1722   During a Holy Week service he feels drawn, for the first time, toward a total conversion.

1723   In a case between the duke of Gravina and the grand-duke of Tuscany, Alphonsus' client, the duke of Gravina, is given an incorrect ruling. Alphonsus leaves the courtroom in disgust never to return.

28 August. While working with the sick in the hospital Alphonsus feels from within a call from God: "Leave everything and give yourself to me." He goes to the altar of Our Lady of Mercy and places the sword of his nobility on it. He has decided to become a priest.

1726   21 September. He is ordained to the priesthood.

1728   Publication of *The Eternal Maxims*.

1730   Alphonsus goes for a period of much needed rest to Amalfi with a few friends. There he begins preaching to the shepherds of Our Lady of the Mountains, in the vicinity of Scala.

His acquaintance with Bishop Falcoia begins and, through him, he meets the Sisters of Scala. Among these nuns is Sister Maria

131

Celeste Costarosa who will be the one to write the Rule for the new order of nuns, the Redemptoristines.

1732 September 9. Alphonsus founds the Congregation of the Fathers of the Holy Savior under the direction of Bishop Falcoia.

The first divisions concerning interpretation of the Rule and the first desertions from the congregation.

The first Redemptorist missions begin.

1736 The Foundation at Ciorani.

1740 Alphonsus, together with all the members takes a vow of perseverance.

1743 Falcoia dies and Alphonsus is elected rector major. He vows not to accept ecclesial responsibilities outside of the congregation.

1744 Foundation at Pagani.

1745 Foundation at Deliceto in Puglia (South east Italy). Alphonsus composes spiritual hymns and publishes *Visits to the Most Blessed Sacrament.*

1747 After failure to receive approval for the congregation by the king of Naples Alphonsus turns to the pope.

1749 February 25. Pope Benedict XIV approves the "Congregation of the Most Holy Redeemer" and confirms Alphonsus as rector for life. The students and novices vow to defend Mary's immaculate conception.

1750 The Redemptoristine nuns receive papal approval.

Publication of *The Glories of Mary.*

1753 Publication of *The Way to Converse Continually and Familiarly with God,* and volume one of *Moral Theology.*

1756 Alphonsus writes *Brief dissertations against the errors of modern unbelievers, the so-called materialist and deists.*

1758 Publication of *Preparation for Death.*

1759 Publication of *On the Great Means of Prayer.*

1760-61 Publication of *The True Spouse of Jesus Christ* (2 volumes).

1762 Appointed Bishop of Saint Agatha of the Goths.

1766 Publication of meditations entitled *The Way of Salvation.*

1768 Publication of *The Practice of the Love of Christ.*

Alphonsus remains crippled from illness and must reduce his activities.

1773 Publishes *Reflections on the Passion of Jesus Christ.*

1775   Alphonsus' resignation as bishop is accepted, he returns to Pagani.

1779   Royal approval of the congregation is finally given but to a changed and distorted rule.
The Redemptorist houses in the Papal States rebel, and some members of the Neapolitan congregations leave to join them.

1780   Pope Pius VI refuses to give papal approval to the Neapolitan houses. He then appoints a superior general for the Congregation in the Papal States. Technically, Alphonsus is out of the approved Congregation.

1785-86 After a period of peace, the dark night of the soul. Alphonsus feels himself rejected even by God. He is helped only by his hope in, "the blood of Jesus Christ who has died for me."

1787   His last year of life is tranquil. He dies August 1 during the noon-time angelus.

1793   The Redemptorists are reunited.

1794   The king of Naples adds his request to many others for the beatification of Alphonsus.

1796   Pope Pius VI confers Alphonsus with the title of Venerable.

1816   September 6. Pope Pius VII declares him Blessed.

1839   May 26. Pope Gregory XVI adds Alphonsus' name to the lists of Saint.

1871   July 7. Pope Pius IX declares him Doctor of the Church, especially for his *Moral Theology*.

1950   April 26. Pope Pius XII proclaims him patron saint of confessors and moralists.

THE PRAYERS OF ST. JOHN OF THE CROSS
Alphonse Ruiz, O.C.D. (ed.)

From the testimony of those who at one time or another found Saint John entranced in prayer, it can be easily concluded that prayer was something connatural to him. In fact, prayer was such an intimate and solid experience that it occupied his whole life and being. There were times when the strength of his intimate relationship with the Lord gave vent to his personal prayer which we find scattered throughout his writings. These fragments are traced in the present collection which shows the width and depth of Saint John's prayer. Thus we can learn from the saint's experience by enjoying and listening to his vibrant and everlasting words.

Series: "Profiles"
ISBN 0-911782-91-5, paper, 128 pp.

THE PRAYERS OF ST. TERESA OF AVILA
Thomas Alvarez, O.C.D. (ed.)   *2d printing*

"Fr. Alvarez has gathered together the written prayers of St. Teresa, using many of her works. The prayers are deeply personal and introduce the reader to the school of prayer which St. Teresa taught her followers. Fr. Alvarez's commentary is often illuminating."

New Heaven/New Earth

"We have all been somewhat embarrassed by the utterances of those in love. But if the one so afflicted is a poet, as Teresa is, what you get is poetry, or perhaps music. One feels almost shy reading these words, as if one has come unannounced upon lovers. . . . Truly a classic."

New Oxford Review

Series "Profiles"
ISBN 0-911782-76-1, paper, 136 pp.

IN SEARCH OF GOD

by W. Herbstrith (with Teresa of Avila, John of the Cross,
Therese of Lisieux, Edith Stein)   2d printing

"Herbstrith's message is not that mysticism is easy, but simply that the
way of mysticism is open to everyone. . . . Her study of this quartet of
Carmelite saints is a vital word on silent prayer and on a spirituality of
belief. The theology is lucid and the biographies are simple, together
opening up a beautiful mystical path through the forest of ordinary
experience."   B.C. Catholic

"[The author] writes to 'present ideas that stem from a tradition of
Christian meditation' shared by the four Carmelite heroes. An introduction to the four, this book might be helpful to those who want to begin to
'stress the fact that mystical life means to abandon oneself to the closeness
of our living God.' "   National Catholic Reporter

"Waltraud Herbstrith, is a Carmelite, also known as Sr. Teresa a Matre
Dei (O.C.D), from Cologne. There's some 'how to' for meditators here,
plus short exegeses of passages and sayings by the above mentioned
mentors."   The Christian Century

"This is a helpful primer on spiritual life. . . ."   Spectrum Review

"Enjoyable reading." Kindred Spirits

Series "Spirituality" — ISBN 0-911728-69-9, paper, 128 pp.

STRONGER THAN HATRED

by St. Maximilian Kolbe   2d printing

"Everybody knows that Father Maximilian Kolbe offered himself in the
place of another prisoner in the concentration camp at Auschwitz. It is
interesting to attempt to discern how that final act of love was prepared
for in these short excerpts from his articles, letters and notebooks of
reflections."   Spiritual Book News

"Stronger than Hatred is a welcome supplement to the body of English-
language work on Maximilian Kolbe. It encapsulates some of his best
epigrammatic writing and elucidates many of the informing moments in
the life of our saint of Auschwitz."   B. C. Catholic

Series "Profiles" — ISBN 0-911782-64-8, paper, 127 pp.